SALVATION:

CHOICE OR CHOSEN?

A PURSUIT OF BIBLICISM

DR. RON TOBIN

THE OLD PATHS PUBLICATIONS, GEORGIA

SALVATION:
CHOICE OR CHOSEN? A PURSUIT OF BIBLICISM

Dr. Ronald Tobin

ISBN: 978-0-9987778-2-5

Individual Copyright © Tomah Baptist Church.

Print Editions: 2018
Printed in the United States of America
All Scripture is from the King James Version

Tomah Baptist Church
1701 Hollister Avenue
Tomah, WI 54660
608-372-2071
Email: info@tomahbaptistchurch.com
Website: TomahBaptistChurch.com

Published by:
The Old Paths Publications, Inc.
142 Gold Flume Way
Cleveland, GA 30528
www.TheOldPathsPublications.com
TOP@theoldpathspublications.com

Foreword

"Calvinism and Reformed Theology are rampant as never before in my fifty-six years of ministry. This fact is true not only in America but in churches in many other places around the world that I have been privileged to preach. Pastor Tobin has done a thorough job in explaining the Calvinist's T.U.L.I.P. theology with an explanation of the proof texts they use to justify their erroneous doctrine. I recommend this book to any serious Christian who is open-minded about knowing the truth."

Evangelist Ron Comfort

Table of Contents

TABLE OF CONTENTS

Acknowledgements

A great debt of gratitude is owed to the patient pastors, missionaries, and professors whom God has used to mold me these many years. They have aided me with my tireless questions and debates.

To the secretaries who tirelessly guided me each step of the way, and patiently persevered through the myriad of edits, I cannot thank you enough!

Most of all, I am appreciative of my dear wife, who from my youth has tirelessly served at my side as my companion. We began our journey of salvation on the same night and had been led by Him across the world, as well as our great Nation.

A Word from the Author

To some people, the title of this work evokes a response of: "Yes, I feel strongly about both points." To most, however, the very idea of either view evokes a passionate response. Whichever viewpoint one holds, their historical positions can be traced back to the second century of Christianity. Most persons on either side are sincere Christians.

The question of the book title came into prominence during the Reformation. The two most noted theologians were John Calvin, who like his fifth-century mentor Augustine sided with "chosen"; and his antagonist Arminius sided with the choice. The truth is they much more agreed than disagreed. The chasm erupted at and after the Council of Dort (1618-1619) when Arminius and his views were condemned to be heretical. Subsequently, those that followed Arminius were hunted down and imprisoned or worse executed.

Arminius' extreme was not simply that a man could freely choose his own destiny and salvation but potentially lose his salvation by choices also. Holiness or righteousness was viewed as somewhat a co-operative effort. To the Calvinist, any such choice for the maintenance of salvation was an enemy of free and sovereign grace. A saving grace only bestowed upon a preselected few down from the ages. Only they hear the call. Only they are regenerated so they will respond with belief. For centuries, Arminius and others argued for a position that man's depravity did not eliminate responsibility, the potentiality of opportunity, or necessity of choice. Both men and followers had errors and

7

extremes of theology; at least as far as their works are concerned. This work is not intended to duplicate the vast volumes written on this subject but rather capsulate.

This work hopes to find a cord of balance. Moreover, while this work attempts to capsulate the arguments or discussion, it is in no way remiss in any part of the subject; rather it focuses on the core issues. This direction should allow any serious student to arrive at a Biblicist position.

The greatest polemical argument that militates against both extremes has always been true REVIVAL. Should Christ tarry His return, may we experience both personal and corporate revival. Maranatha!

Chapter 1: Introduction

Those considered four or five-point Calvinists are not always harsh, unloving or non-evangelistic witnesses. It also cannot be said those who oppose the Calvinist system are Arminians or so-called "Calminiast" or less intellectual. There is enough arrogance, pride, and misrepresentation on all sides.

Most of those individuals have gone toward Calvinism because of the influence of trending blogs, or because it is the newest fad for younger adults, its appeal of supposed intellectualism, and even a hands-off attitude toward *separation* in more modern Calvinists. For this reason, this work is written to help two groups of believers.

The first group is the sincere students in our churches that are separation-minded soul-winners, and Dispensationalists in pursuit of the Lost. It is secondly for the younger pastors or seminary students perhaps wavering but still looking for answers. I hope to encourage both groups of individuals to proclaim a new mantle or title—*Biblicists* (See Ch. 2 on Terms).

It is past time that we shake off the archaic labels of Arminians, Calvinists or "Calminians." This choice must be made the same as our forefathers—the Baptists and Fundamentalists had to do. The position put forth in this work is in the strictest sense—both balanced in logic and theology, as well as Scripture. It is my desire some of our strict Calvinist brethren might ponder some of the truths put forth in this book.

REVIVALS

The great revivals of the 1700's, 1800's, and the early 1900's were often led by those considered Calvinists, Non-Calvinists and Arminians. Out of those revival periods, there developed a fusion of thought which led to a revival of Dispensationalism and the Pre-Millennial views. At the same time, old-line denominations with their reformed and covenant theology fell prey to Modernism and Liberalism (the rejection of core Christian doctrines). The Separatist remnants were called "Fundamentalist" by their detractors for defending the fundamentals of the faith (core doctrines). They came from a variety of theological persuasions. They were focused and unified in their defense of historic biblical Christianity.

THE NEED

Today in our splintering biblical lives one of the movements affecting Christianity and revival is a resurgence of modern Calvinism. It is marked by its leaders and proponents especially online. Their views range from sincerity to arrogant, intolerant intellectual elitism. What needs to be answered is three-fold:

1.) Does it matter?
2.) What is the truth?
3.) What are the consequences?

This work should systematically answer those questions from a pastoral perspective.

Another need or perspective is to find if there is a balance which neither tips toward Calvinism or Arminianism. For instance, can the aided will choose or reject God's salvation without the choice being a "self-work" or righteousness? Does man's depravity render him helplessly incapable of choosing Christ even when hearing God's Word and under the general conviction of the Holy Spirit, (if, in fact, the Holy Spirit even bothers)? Does man need an unrevealed X-factor of a selective or exclusive call? Does that mean that all others without that internal flame or mark or other identifiers are hopelessly damned? Is it factual and biblical that he who is foreordained to Salvation must first be regenerated (spiritually renewed) so that he can be enabled to make the choice that otherwise would be against his will? Could that also occur years before he chooses or never chooses? Does that even make sense or is it just philosophical sophistry or theological gymnastics?

Moreover, what is the great difference between the Calvinist and Arminians notion of "Perseverance of the Saints"? They seem to both arrive at the same fence posts of proving Salvation by righteous works. Why not accept "Eternal Security" (a more modern term) because of redemptions legal full estate and the continuation of regeneration? Why is this not the security and biblical decree in the predestination of those who have been saved?

Ephesians 1:4-10 According as he hath chosen us in him before the foundation of the world, that we should be holy and without blame before him in love: Having predestinated us unto the adoption of children by Jesus Christ to himself, according to the good pleasure of his will, To the praise of the glory of his grace, wherein he hath made us accepted in the beloved. In whom we have redemption through his blood, the forgiveness of sins, according to the riches of his grace; Wherein he hath abounded toward us in all wisdom and prudence; Having made known unto us the mystery of his will, according to his good pleasure which he hath purposed in himself: That in the dispensation of the fullness of times he might gather together in one all things in Christ, both which are in heaven, and which are on earth; even in him.

Finally, questions ultimately must begin with our Sovereign God. Are either Calvinists or Arminians totally correct in their statements about God? Does either view go off the beam a little? Is the Calvinist explanation consistent with God's revealed nature or plan? Is the Calvinist explanation of God's exclusionary love biblical and consistent? What about the Calvinist claim about who's whosoever?

There are serious questions with which the average sincere pastor or Christian is left. There are glaring logical but unscriptural promises or statements by the Calvinist system. Perhaps this is due to originating in the Reformed or Covenant system. That may also be why the modern alliance of Calvinism with Dispensationalist tends to border mere tolerance or theological schizophrenia.

Whatever the problems are in all systems, we want to arrive at a truly biblical and balanced truth.

Chapter 2: Knowing the Players

(A Brief History of Persons & Terms)

This chapter will briefly introduce the important events or persons; as well as important doctrinal terms. A general definition will be considered unless there is a difference of views.

Historical Persons

Augustine of Hippo

Augustine was born Aurelius Augustinus on November 13, 354 A.D. in what would be modern Algeria. His father was a pagan Roman officer and his mother, Monica, a godly Christian. He was well educated in classical Greek philosophy and law. As a young adult, he lived a riotous life. Later because of his mother's prayers and testimony, he converted to Christianity. He would move to Hippo, Africa and became a bishop. He is often credited with being one of the main founders of early Catholic doctrine.

Augustine's theology, though sometimes in conflict with later Roman Catholic doctrine, became the foundation for much of John Calvin's views. Later Augustine would become the defender of the faith for Rome against the Pelagian heresies and persecutor of Donatist (early Baptists) for their views insubordinate to the Roman Bishop. He was also used as a missionary educator to Britain briefly after Rome's fall in 410 A.D. He would produce his work *The City of God*.

John Calvin

Calvin (1509-1564) was one of the main leaders of the Reformation movement and perhaps most influential. He was a contemporary of Luther, Zwingli, Bullinger, Beza, and Melanchthon. Most of them were Swiss. Calvin was born July 10, 1509, in Noyon, France. Martin Luther was already twenty-five years old at the time of Calvin's birth (Vance, 7). While Calvin was an exceptional scholar, little is known about his conversion, except that he was heavily influenced by the times. He was educated at the Church of Rome and School of Law.

Calvin was both an enigma and contradiction. He proclaimed Free Grace and murdered his opponents. In 1536, he assumed a pastorate in Geneva until 1538, when the town council of Geneva banished him for a season. Calvin later returned and used the State to enforce church (Christian) lifestyles upon the citizens, thus fusing a Protestant State Church. The rules were harsh at best, which is why he was referred to as "The Geneva Dictator" (Ibid, 84).

While Calvin wrote much, he is best known for his *Institutes of the Christian Religion*. It was that bulwark of God, the Trinity, and Salvation which so influenced people through the Ages. In fact, many of his followers took his view further than where he, such as the acrostic T.U.L.I.P. (though I think he would subscribe to it) (Ibid, 79).

James Arminius

Arminius was born October 10, 1560, at Oudewater, Holland, and died at age forty-nine in 1609. He was four years old when Calvin died in 1564, and

14

thus, never debated Calvin. He was initially enrolled at the University of Marburg in Marburg Germany, the First Protestant University until the Spanish army invaded the city. He would later, in 1576, attend the University of Leiden, a Protestant school where he would distinguish himself (Vance, 123). Arminius had his theological training at the school Calvin founded. He even recommended reading Calvin's *Institutes of the Christian Religion.*

Overall, Arminius' theology was conservative. He considered all sixty-six books of the Bible infallible. He was more of a humanist of the times since he was a staunch anti-Catholic—similar to Calvin. He believed mankind to be "hopelessly lost," and by himself incapable of doing good in his will or self; thus, he needed salvation by Christ alone. He believed in justification by faith like Luther or Calvin. He further believed in a security of believers, and rejected believers could fall away from faith or salvation. Like other reformers, he sprinkled infants and rejected the Anabaptist. Unlike Calvin, he was tolerant of those with whom he disagreed. (Ibid., 127-132).

Arminius rejected the supralapsarian Calvinist view of Predestination and wrote a treatise with twenty points refuting them. To him, Predestination was not the foundation of Salvation. He found the view to be repugnant to the Gospel and nature of God. To Arminius, the Calvinistic ideas of both supralapsarianism and sublapsarianism made God's Providence the Author of Sin. To him, the Believer is predestined to Eternal Life when one repents and believes. Furthermore, he believed that one's will had sufficient ability to do good if assisted by divine grace to perform it and required regeneration.

That idea greatly differed from Pelagius' view (Salvation by man's effort) or Thomas Aquinas' views of human perfection through the mind. Arminius rejected the idea of Irresistible Grace because of Scriptural proof and that it was not a philosophical system.

Arminius, however, while interpreting some Scriptural passages, believed it was possible for a believer to quit believing, and thus fall away. So according to that idea, assurance of salvation was only reached by subjective means, if the Believer kept responding to Grace and the Holy Spirit. That was where he found himself in a dilemma. Salvation still depends upon, in some way, the Believer's will, and not a legally binding contract. That view in some ways contradicted his view of Predestination and Adoption. He was, however, reformed in his thinking, and in no way Pelagian (Studebaker, 13-14).

The Synod or Council of Dort

The Synod of Dort was a national council that took place from 1618-1619, in the town of Dordrecht, in the Netherlands. It was held by the Dutch Reformed Church initially to discuss the Arminians' views. Those who objected to Calvin's and Beza's views published their objection in 1610 in a paper called *The Remonstrants*. During that meeting, they debated thirteen of those Remonstrants at Dort in 1618. From that meeting, the five points of Calvinism were put forth (referred to as the T.U.L.I.P.).

Another sad note in history was the false accusations against the followers of James Arminius. Many were hunted down and imprisoned, while some were even killed (Vance, 149-150).

Chapter 3: Relevant Words/Terms

Grace

"The free, unmerited favor of God, as manifested in the salvation of sinners and bestowal of blessings" (Baker's Evangelical Dictionary of Biblical Theology, 1996).

The Arminians would accept the above definition, but believe since all men received a call from the Lord, anyone could resist. Additionally, they might contend a Believer who does not yield the call of the Holy Spirit could fall from Grace. To the Calvinist, only a definite select number of sinners were chosen before Creation and predetermined for salvation. For them, Salvation never can be lost. They believe that that they alone receive the effective call of Salvation.

The Roman Church believes in salvation by Grace must be perpetuated by human effort and therefore merit grace. The Biblicist sees as the Calvinist; that grace is free and unmerited and that it encompasses the whole dimension of salvation. It affects our being drawn to Christ, Who provides Salvation and uses the drawing power of the Holy Spirit unto all men. It can and is rejected by men. When yielded to it, Grace enables men for their regeneration and sanctification. Grace is the instrument to bring the believer into the presence of Jesus.

John 12:32 And I, if I be lifted up from the earth, will draw all men unto me.

Regeneration

Man's spiritually lost estate is regenerated upon one's faith alone in the finished work of Christ on the cross. No amount of good works or keeping of the Law can regenerate the heart. It is to bring back to life that which is spiritually dead.

> *Ephesians 2:1-6 And you hath he quickened, who were dead in trespasses and sins; Wherein in time past ye walked according to the course of this world, according to the prince of the power of the air, the spirit that now worketh in the children of disobedience: Among whom also we all had our conversation in times past in the lusts of our flesh, fulfilling the desires of the flesh and of the mind; and were by nature the children of wrath, even as others. But God, who is rich in mercy, for his great love wherewith he loved us, Even when we were dead in sins, hath quickened us together with Christ, (by grace ye are saved;) And hath raised us up together, and made us sit together in heavenly places in Christ Jesus:*

It is the new birth or experience of being *Born Again*. The Lord's rich grace is the cause of rebirth. It is the display of resurrection power in the sinner (GotQuestions.org, 2017). Regeneration as a power and process has a definite beginning for the convert without end. The Calvinist can see the event (Regeneration / New Birth) affected in a person even years before they believe because they have been elected and predestined. The question is: "Does it occur before to enable them; simultaneously when the will, in hopeless abandonment, yields the Holy Spirit; or after belief was exercised?" While there can be a danger in declaring regeneration occurs as a response to faith, there is an equal danger in declaring it preceding faith with no time limit. Even then, is it an hour, a twinkling of an eye or years before? Certainly Titus 3:5 refutes Romanism as it can never be by righteous works.

Romans 3:5 But if our unrighteousness commend the righteousness of God, what shall we say? Is God unrighteous who taketh vengeance? (I speak as a man)

Justification

One source defines justification as: "the act, process, or state of being justified by God" or "vindication" *(*Merriam-webster.com, 2017*)*. It is a legal declaration or findings as "an act of God whereby humankind is made or accounted just in Christ, or free from guilt or penalty of sin by faith" (Dictionary.com, 2017). That act not only sets a person free from Sin's charge but then declares them righteous in Christ.

Romans 10:10 For with the heart man believeth unto righteousness; and with the mouth confession is made unto salvation.

2 Corinthians 5:21 For he hath made him to be sin for us, who knew no sin; that we might be made the righteousness of God in him.

God sees Christ's own righteousness when he looks upon us and sees us perfect in Christ and declares us righteous – justified (GotQuestions.org, 2017). That becomes the Bible believer's source of hope and assurance—and not in His persevering. There is no double jeopardy with God!

Redemption

Redemption is a term and practice originally in the Old Testament prior to and during The Law. People, property, or things can be redeemed. Generally, the term meant to set someone or something free from bonds or slavery, buying back something lost. From a biblical perspective, redemption was also a legal term. It always requires a payment. In the New Testament, Christ's person and blood became the ransom price for sinful man. (Elwell, Walter A. "Entry for 'Redeem, Redemption'". "Evangelical Dictionary of Theology," 1997.).

> *Galatians 3:10 For as many as are of the works of the law are under the curse: for it is written, Cursed is every one that continueth not in all things which are written in the book of the law to do them.*

> *Galatians 3:13 Christ hath redeemed us from the curse of the law, being made a curse for us: for it is written, Cursed is every one that hangeth on a tree:*

> *Colossians 1:14 In whom we have redemption through his blood, even the forgiveness of sins:*

Again, a nuance of the Calvinist who cannot support *Limited Atonement* will reroute that unscriptural concept with *Particular Redemption.* In other words, it is not simply the Believer benefiting, or any potential *whosoever will,* but only those elected in eternity past and predestined to salvation. It still is the same old philosophical sophistry and gymnastics. It must also be noted, that while a potential benefit unclaimed is never realized, it is still a potential benefit to all it was offered. That is not universal salvation but a universal offer.

Mark 16:15 And he said unto them, Go ye into all the world, and preach the gospel to every creature.

Acts 10:34 Then Peter opened his mouth, and said, Of a truth I perceive that God is no respecter of persons:

Romans 10:12 For there is no difference between the Jew and the Greek: for the same Lord over all is rich unto all that call upon him.

2 Corinthians 5:14-15 For the love of Christ constraineth us; because we thus judge, that if one died for all, then were all dead: And that he died for all, that they which live should not henceforth live unto themselves, but unto him which died for them, and rose again.

1 Timothy 2:1-4 I exhort therefore, that, first of all, supplications, prayers, intercessions, and giving of thanks, be made for all men; For kings, and for all that are in authority; that we may lead a quiet and peaceable life in all godliness and honesty. For this is good and acceptable in the sight of God our Saviour; Who will have all men to be saved, and to come unto the knowledge of the truth.

1 John 2:2 And he is the propitiation for our sins: and not for ours only, but also for the sins of the whole world.

21

Revelation 22:17 And the Spirit and the bride say, Come. And let him that heareth say, Come. And let him that is athirst come. And whosoever will, let him take the water of life freely.

Atonement

Merriam Webster defines *atonement* as "reparation for an offense or an injury. The reconciliation of God and humankind through the sacrificial death of Jesus Christ" (Merriam-Webster.com, 2017). Another source stated that "God has provided a way for humankind to come back into harmonious relation with Him" (Baker's Evangelical Dictionary of Biblical Theology, 1996). In the Old Testament, it was a temporary covering. In the New Testament, Christ, the permanent solution has once and for all paid the ultimate sacrifice for Man's sin for all Eternity. Christ was what the temporary solution for which the Law was waiting.

Colossians 2:17 Which are a shadow of things to come; but the body is of Christ.

Hebrews 8:5a Who serve unto the example and shadow of heavenly things, as Moses was admonished of God when he was about to make the tabernacle: ...

On the general statement Biblicists, Arminians, and Calvinists agree; however, the devil is the detail. Of course, Rome can never admit this since it militated against their mass and priesthood. We all agree that it was only applied to the Elect known by God's foreknowledge from eternity past.

1 Peter 1:2 Elect according to the foreknowledge of God the Father, through sanctification of the Spirit, unto obedience and sprinkling of the blood of Jesus Christ: Grace unto you, and peace, be multiplied.

The problem occurs as to whom and when was a person elected. The Calvinist sees the atonement limited to his defined elect and predestined. The Biblicist sees the atonement for all mankind so that some people will respond. Without the legal eradication of the moral, spiritual and one day, physical effects of sin, no one could benefit. This is a moral, spiritual and physical reality. Either Christ was the "lamb that taketh away the sin of the world", so the Believer benefits—or no one at all.

John 1:29 The next day John seeth Jesus coming unto him, and saith, Behold the Lamb of God, which taketh away the sin of the world.

Elect

Simply put, elect(ion) means to be chosen or singled out. For Christians, the choice is one of the three possible answers or a combination. One idea states a person is elected to salvation before Creation, according to God's secret purposes. Thus by default or design, all others are predestined to a deserved Hell. Meanwhile, some Christians insist that election was in Eternity Past, therefore, those who actually will choose are foreknown by God.

For the Calvinist, the notion that God foreknew those who would choose is *anathema*. They believe that choice limits God's foreknowledge or makes it dependent on man's response. God's foreknowledge in Calvinism is often equivalent to a predestined election. God purposely and selectively knows one over another. That was how Calvinists explained 1 Peter 1:2 and the word *foreknowledge*. That is how all things come to be in existence for salvation. God selectively chooses what must be. That foreknowledge becomes the balance of His omniscience.

> *1 Peter 1:2 Elect according to the foreknowledge of God the Father, through sanctification of the Spirit, unto obedience and sprinkling of the blood of Jesus Christ: Grace unto you, and peace, be multiplied.*

Other Believers, however, see that notion in part making God a master chess player or puppeteer. Election is not to make one a believer, but to purpose that the Believer would be positionally in Christ, and to be Holy and blameless.

> *Ephesians 1:4 According as he hath chosen us in him before the foundation of the world, that we should be holy and without blame before him in love:*

God has never in Scripture said to elect men to salvation, but rather to His purposes, sanctification, and glorification. Certainly, the Patriarchs were called and chosen. Moses, Israel, the Apostles, and Paul—all had to respond willingly.

Predestination

One commentary defined Predestination in this manner:

"God has a purpose that is determined long before it is brought to pass. It implies that God is infinitely capable of planning and then bringing about what he has planned...The people in the New Testament, like Israel in the Old Testament has a destiny to fulfill. Both Old and New Testament speak of individuals being predestined to fulfill a divine purpose" (Baker's Evangelical Dictionary of Biblical Theology, 1996).

Here are some examples of Predestination from the Scriptures:

- Jeremiah was called and set apart in his mother's womb for a divine purpose.

  Jeremiah 1:5 Before I formed thee in the belly I knew thee; and before thou camest forth out of the womb I sanctified thee, and I ordained thee a prophet unto the nations.

- Jacob and Esau, while in their mother's womb had a destiny.

  Genesis 25:23 And the LORD said unto her, Two nations are in thy womb, and two manner of people shall be separated from thy bowels; and the one people shall be stronger than the other people; and the elder shall serve the younger.

- Paul declared his destiny was from birth.

  Galatians 1:15-16 But when it pleased God, who separated me from my mother's womb, and called me by his grace, To reveal his Son in me, that I might preach him among the heathen; immediately I conferred not with flesh and blood:

So predestination in the Old and New Testament is for a purpose and viewed after one responded to God's offer. One is a free moral agent limited or perverted by sin, yet aided by God. That concept is not understood as a mechanistic fixed system like some version of Christian evolution or Kharma.

In the New Testament, the purpose of our destiny predetermined is to be conformed to:

- Christ's image

    Romans 8:29 For whom he did foreknow, he also did predestinate to be conformed to the image of his Son, that he might be the firstborn among many brethren.

- Adoption

    Ephesians 1:5-6 Having predestinated us unto the adoption of children by Jesus Christ to himself, according to the good pleasure of his will, To the praise of the glory of his grace, wherein he hath made us accepted in the beloved.

- An Inheritance or to be to the "Praise of His Glory

    Ephesians 1:11-12 In whom also we have obtained an inheritance, being predestinated according to the purpose of him who worketh all things after the counsel of his own will: That we should be to the praise of his glory, who first trusted in Christ.

A believer must avoid assumptions that those verses refer to persons and not purposes. Assumptions will damage one's strict biblical view. That is why we should always strive to be Biblicists first.

Total Depravity

Total depravity is not a term coined by Reformers, especially Calvin, but originated centuries earlier with Augustine. One source states it is "...a Theological term derived from the Augustinian concept of original sin..." Rather it means that even the good that a person may intend is faulty in its premise, false in its motive, and weak in its implementations...every person born into the world is enslaved to the service of sin...and is utterly unable to choose to follow God, refrain from evil, or accept the gift of salvation as it is offered" (Canons of Dordt, 2017).

All Protestants—whether reformed or others— would accept that definition. There may be some exceptions among Lutherans, Methodists, or Pentecostal - Charismatics. There is also a twisted concept added by imposing infant baptism as a promise or initiation to Christianity, or a replacement for legalistic circumcision.

The differences among Arminians, Calvinists or Biblicists are sometimes more than just terminology. The Calvinist believes in an absolute, incapable will to choose for anyone apart from their notion of Irresistible Grace foisted upon the predestined (decreed) Elect. The Arminians promote Prevenient Grace, which some early Catholic theologians promoted. Arminian Free Will Baptist theologian Robert E. Picirilli says that the word "prevenient" in prevenient grace comes from an archaic English usage meaning "anticipating," "coming before," or "preceding." Picirilli says that a good synonym for "prevenient grace" is "enabling grace," as it *enables* sinful mankind to believe (58). Wesleyans or Free Will Baptists,

Nazarenes, and others tend to follow that view. Today it is referred to as *preceding grace*.

The Calvinist calls such preceding grace *Semipelagian*. However, the Calvinists still have their own form of prevenient grace—they just call it *regeneration prior to salvation*. The Calvinist's views of man's fallen estate (depravity) are no different from Satan's and his demons. To them, a fall is a fall, and depravity is depravity. There is, however, a difference between the two created beings and the Fall. The angelic order was first, more powerful, and immediately more privileged in their relationship with the Godhead. There is a difference, therefore, in their souls or bodies (immaterial). Those that fell or did not fall never could procreate, so they are fixed in number. Those that fell cannot nor will not be redeemed. Redemption's pardon is specifically for Man with the whole creation benefiting. In short, man's depravity is different; and by the fact of Salvation's acceptance is not a total inability—especially with the convicting influence of the Holy Spirit.

> *John 16:7-11 Nevertheless I tell you the truth; It is expedient for you that I go away: for if I go not away, the Comforter will not come unto you; but if I depart, I will send him unto you. And when he is come, he will reprove the world of sin, and of righteousness, and of judgment: Of sin, because they believe not on me; Of righteousness, because I go to my Father, and ye see me no more; Of judgment, because the prince of this world is judged.*

Biblicist

Every Christian from every denomination will proclaim himself a *Biblicist*. That is true for Arminians, Calvinists, and Catholics. In fact, even cultists will loudly protest. So what constitutes a Biblicist?

First, they believe the Bible to be God's final authority (and He possesses it). Therefore, the Bible is approached and understood <u>inductively</u>. That approach is important because God's Word interprets itself, comparing Scripture with Scripture.

> *Acts 17:11 These were more noble than those in Thessalonica, in that they received the word with all readiness of mind, and searched the scriptures daily, whether those things were so.*

They approach the Bible as a whole knowing God's recorded revelation is progressively imparted through the Ages. Each period or dispensation reveals more of His plan. That is why which Bible translation is most accurate is pertinent to the process.

A Biblicist cannot approach the Word through the tainted glasses of denominationalism or any other preconceived notions (deductive study). Objectivity produces accuracy! Conclusions must only be decided after painstaking efforts are made to understand terms, definitions, sentences and finally context. Literal remains literal, and symbolism is a symbolic reference—whether immediate to the situation or prophetically. While we can draw many applications, there can only be one truth or interpretation.

> *Ephesians 4:3-6 Endeavouring to keep the unity of the Spirit in the bond of peace. There is one body, and one Spirit, even as ye are called in one hope of your calling; One Lord, one faith, one baptism, One God and Father of all, who is above all, and through all, and in you all.*

That too often was not consistently so with the Reformers or Protestants. Our nature's limits or prejudices war against us. Modern attempts at Biblicism are also interrupted in the blogosphere. Hence a Biblicist must be a person who deeply reads and researches the Bible with an analytical framework. "What is God teaching?" is their creed? They must also be bathed in prayer. Finally, they cannot make assertions, assumptions, or interpretations that God has not.

A Biblicist cannot rely on what is commonly referred to as *the Aristotelian approach* or *scientific method.* In that system, they begin with a hypothesis (assumption), then test that hypothesis. They arrive at a theory until reaching a law or absolute. That may sound good, except one begins with assumptions and seeks the Scripture or meanings to validate those assumptions. What if those assumptions were wrong and cannot stand up to scrutiny? What if we have opposing views or seemingly difficult Scriptural statements? Does one default to their notions? Should we go back to Rome, as some in New Covenant beliefs are doing?

When confronted, the Biblicist will correct themselves or system. So, if a Biblicist reads that God gives people a will to choose and a choice to make for salvation, they conclude humanity can choose. If the Bible uses the term elect or other related terms, then they are obligated to find meaning, truth, and balance in each of the uses. Since Scripture renders one's ability and necessity to choose Christ as an absolute, then the process (Election, Predestination, Regeneration) cannot mean the abrogation of one's absolute to choose. That is why a true Calvinist cannot be a complete Biblicist.

In summary, the Biblicist's position is necessary for accurately approaching the discussion of Salvation: Choice or Chosen?

All of the previously mentioned terms and uses will be touched upon in the following chapters.

Chapter 4: In the Beginning God...

Whatever theological system from which we come, God must not only be at the center, He must also be at the beginning and ending. Either God is all (Sovereign) or not at all. There can be no room for gray or man's autonomy. There is no such thing as a Theological Libertarian. That is the place in which the old Deist or the Theistic Evolutionists slid. Whether a person calls themselves a Calvinist, Arminian, or Biblicist—everything should originate with God.

Every Bible college student or even church member understands the simple truth about God being supreme and sovereign over His creation. What comes into question is not whether God is supreme and sovereign but how does He express that? He can do whatever he wants. We know He is good and never does anything capricious or impulsively. Everything has a purpose within His plan.

> *Psalms 33:6 By the word of the LORD were the heavens made; and all the host of them by the breath of his mouth.*

> *Psalms 33:13 The LORD looketh from heaven; he beholdeth all the sons of men.*

> *Psalms 115:3 But our God is in the heavens: he hath done whatsoever he hath pleased.*

One Calvinist, B.B. Warfield, put it this way, "The Calvinist is the man who sees God behind all phenomena and in all that occurs recognizes the hand of God, working out His will" (Meeter, 35). Calvin even stated:

"God is deemed omnipotent not because He can act...but because governing heaven and earth by His providence, He so over ruled all things that nothing happens without His counsel...He, as it were, holds the helm, and over rules all events" (174-175).

No true Bible believer could ever disagree with the autonomous power or governance of God. His providence is not idle, as it is actively involved in the intricacies of the affairs of men. As Nebuchadnezzar observed:

> *Daniel 4:17 This matter is by the decree of the watchers, and the demand by the word of the holy ones: to the intent that the living may know that the most High ruleth in the kingdom of men, and giveth it to whomsoever he will, and setteth up over it the basest of men.*

> *Daniel 4:35 And all the inhabitants of the earth are reputed as nothing: and he doeth according to his will in the army of heaven, and among the inhabitants of the earth: and none can stay his hand, or say unto him, What doest thou?*

God who lives in the Eternal Present has a plan which He has and is actively engaged in the operation. God decreed the existence of His creation, planned for the Fall and has secured the plan's fulfillment. That is sovereign power and providential oversight. So, where can there be an objection to that? There is none, except when we seek His character in Salvation's fulfillment. Shall we limit His power, knowledge, or nature of love, grace, and mercy, so that it is capsulated within finite understanding?

Disregarding all the defensive platitudes from any position, one could ask, "Is the unfathomable, infinite and unconditional love of God only extended to an extreme minority of preselected? Is that the exhibition and nature of *agape* or divine justice or holiness?" David Hunt asked that very question is his work *What Love is This.* He aptly stated that in Calvin's entire *Institute of the Christian Religion:* "There is not one mention of God's love for the lost!" (192). Calvin's God can love only the Elect. "And how can it be said that God loves those whom He predestined to eternal torment before they were born?" (Ibid). In the Calvinist's mindset, God's selective love is all that is necessary to prove God's love. So one had to accept that idea without question. That question was posed because of the seemingly contradictory and irrational statements about God's love or goodness toward the lost. Such contradictions seem to plague those holding to a strict Calvinist position. They are to themselves safe within their own logic, but not so when universal logic is applied—especially of the "If, then or but Scripture states...type. That is the dilemma of the logical conclusion of Calvinists love. They all hold to the idea of a *duo predestination* (dual predestination) position when declaring the sovereignty and decreeing God.

But wait! Is not God sovereign enough to work together all of Man's lost condition that affects his abilities and the Lord's call and command to believe on Christ Jesus? Does humankind have an active and capable ability to choose or yield to God if promoted by the Holy Spirit according to the method declared in Scripture?

God's Word states:

John 16:8 And when he is come, he will reprove the world of sin, and of righteousness, and of judgment.

Romans 10:17 So then faith cometh by hearing, and hearing by the word of God.

Hebrews 4:12 For the word of God is quick, and powerful, and sharper than any twoedged sword, piercing even to the dividing asunder of soul and spirit, and of the joints and marrow, and is a discerner of the thoughts and intents of the heart.

To summarize those thoughts: all things are of and for the Omnipotent, Omniscient, and Sovereign God. He does love His Creation and gives all humans legitimate opportunity to accept Him on His terms. Less than that would limit His nature. His Spirit is not required to regenerate man first (save) so that he will call on Jesus (as true Calvinists believe). That would limit the sovereign God's plan or ability to utilize man's limitations in the choice of salvation. To find the outcome by the Holy Spirit regenerating a preselect one to choose makes God the one choosing God, and man—a controlled, passive participant. However, to allow God to work out the How, and not simply Who, before Creation is His purpose in Christ. That concession allows God to be supremely sovereign, even if that is a secret to us. Understanding that idea does not limit or alter His foreknowledge in any way.

Ephesians 1:4 According as he hath chosen us in him before the foundation of the world, that we should be holy and without blame before him in love:

Deuteronomy 29:29 The secret things belong unto the LORD our God: but those things which are revealed belong unto us and to our children for ever, that we may do all the words of this law.

The upcoming chapters will take a look at the concepts of human depravity, God's love, human election, predestination, and other important fundamentals. Hopefully, through this discussion, we will free God's sovereignty from the Calvinist limitations or misrepresentations, as well as from Arminians or others of similar mindsets.

Arminians and Calvinists, as well as other Reformers, were seeking to escape the clutches of the Holy Roman Empire. That tended to influence their thought and behavior. While it is too easy to view the Past with twenty-first-century spectacles, to get a more accurate understanding, one should strive to avoid that tendency. Neither should a person condone the vile excesses of the Reformers with those who disagreed with them.

Chapter 5: Essential Calvinism

Essential to the Calvinist system is the keeping of God Supreme to His Creation. What also seemed to be essential to the Calvinist was the extreme lack of value of humanity. That value is essential to the understanding of Grace's work as well as the limitations of the atonement and redemption of humanity. That offer extends to God's love reserved only for the Elect.

Below is a short understanding of the Calvinist's system in their line of logic or *Philo-theology*.

1. God in eternity past, purposed in His own heart for His own good pleasure, a plan that included Creation, Redemption and the Ages to Come.
2. He decreed what would be, and fixed the outcomes, and predestined for Salvation those who would or would not be saved (the Elect).
3. He elects (selects) for Salvation only those predestined (decreed) because of the irreversible inability of humans to choose the righteous good. At best, they only choose the lesser evils. *Note: All parents still love a defiant, rebel child and feel the pain.*
4. He then purposely and selectively foreknows the Elected, and not merely in advance of their choice, because He already made their choice.
5. He then fixes or secures their irreversible salvation so they, by works, *persevere* in faith as evidenced by their "righteous works" and surrender to a "Lordship Salvation."
6. At the appropriate moment of time, God gives the Elect a second non-universal call; (*efficacious*) "a

fanning of a flame" or a secret imprint, to which only the Elect can hear or respond.

7. The Holy Spirit then regenerates the not-yet believing Elect, thus allowing their will to believe or choose Christ, as the Holy Spirit makes that choice through the unbeliever.

Therefore, according to the Calvinist's theory, regeneration must precede and prompt unto Salvation. That belief is due to their view of depravity and the human will. To the Calvinists, Salvation cannot happen simultaneously with regeneration. So the Sinner's (elect) choice is in part or whole, surreal, but not truly real. It was not merely an aided choice, but the choice which the elect merely consents to after the fact. Stephen Charnock likened it to hounds fixating on one fox, chasing it up a tree and all the while barking. Inevitably the fox, out of fear and exhaustion, dropped from the tree onto the hounds. That is all the choice Calvinists attribute a few people to have. Some people may take longer, but all whom God is fixed upon have to surrender. They cannot or will not resist.

8. A modern nuance incorporated into this system when confronted with the harshness even toward their own family or children was added to their sophistry. Children of the Elect were automatically included in the Election by virtue of their relationship to their parents. (Somebody should have told Israel!)

For the Calvinist, to do less than that would contradict Grace or leave it for Chance, and therefore, God's Eternal Plan for failure. Below are several statements by Calvinists (or those with Reformed and Covenant Theology views):

> If Unconditional Election is true; that is, if God unconditionally determined the eternal destiny of every member of the human race by a sovereign, eternal, all-encompassing decree, then certainly infants are included. For all men, whether "elect" or "reprobate," have first to be born as an infant before attaining adulthood. The problem, however, is what happens when an infant dies. The question of whether children who die in infancy are counted among the "elect" has plagued Calvinism since the very beginning. The mention of "elect infants, dying in infancy" in the Westminster Confession of Faith, has especially troubled the Calvinists. In fact, the Cumberland Presbyterians were so troubled by the phrase that in 1813 they revised the wording of this article in the Westminster Confession.
>
> Regarding the possibility that some infants who die are among the "reprobate," Spurgeon comments: "Among the gross falsehoods which have been uttered against the Calvinists proper, is the wicked calumny that we *hold the damnation of little infants*. A baser lie was never uttered. There may have existed somewhere, in some corner of the earth, a miscreant who would dare to say that there were infants in hell, but I have never met

with him, nor have I met with a man who ever saw such a person." So even though election is supposed to be sovereign and unconditional, Calvinists, as a rule, would insist that all children who die in infancy are part of the "elect."*(Vance, 397)*

Vance accurately portrayed the Calvinist duality of thought. While the Calvinist believer cannot admit non-Elect into Heaven, they also cannot omit unsaved children who are undetermined in their election. When considering their own children, Calvinists not only approach heresy, but incredulity.

On the following page, there is a basic chart depicting the Calvinist view.

Fall of Man - Sin

Sovereign Grace Salvation

ETERNAL SALVATION
Free will to make a spiritual choice at some point

Elect Sinner Regenerated to Repent

Efficacious call to only the elect

Atonement for only the elect

Mankind helpless & hopeless sinners

Eternal Damnation
The Place of all Non-Elect & Predestined

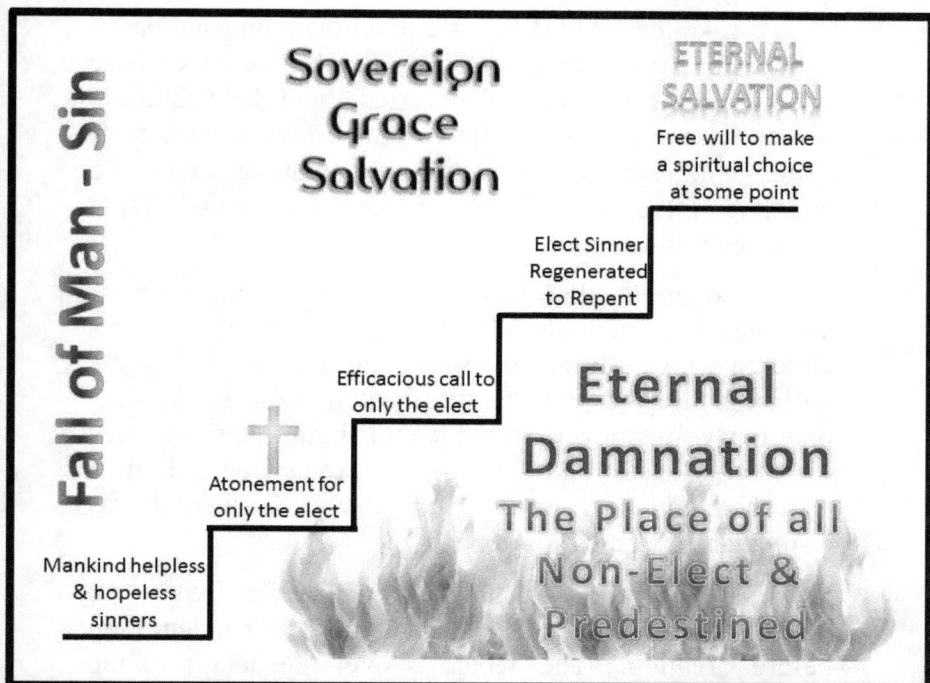

Eternity Past
God in Eternity Past
➤Purposeful Plan
➤Decrees
➤Chose some for Salvation

Calvinist Grace
God prior to creation by decrees
➤ Elected a few to be saved in the future
➤ He foreknew the elect over others.
The others He chose not to know or elect.
➤ Those God elected to salvation He predestined (decreed) their eternal destiny.

Like the T.U.L.I.P. system, all the points are based on a philosophical logic first. Point eight was added later to confront those individuals worried about their children. It was meant to answer the logical problem with their system with regard to the questions: "What happens to the children of the elect? How can they ever know? What about rebellious children?"

So in Jonathan Edward's day, the Congregationalist had a partial church membership for the Elect's children who were not quite ready to give in (That issue will be addressed in more detail later in the book). As previously mentioned, the idea of infant baptism was essential to Reformed Theology as well. For Calvin, it was their entrance circumcision, and for Luther, it was also in case babies *could* repent.

No Biblicist could ever disagree with our Sovereign God having a plan for Creation or redemption before Creation. The debate is over the details of the Who, How, When, and Why of Salvation. Furthermore, there is also debate regarding the interpretation of specific scriptures.

Finally, the debate also continues over the nature and character of God, as well as His decrees. Some differ on the question of whether God's offer of salvation is intended for anyone or only a select secret group? Does *all* mean *all*, or does *whosoever* mean *whosoever*? In fact, is God's love or salvation offer sincere if the non-Elect cannot respond, yet are damned for not doing so?

For the Calvinist, this demonstration is God's love and mercy because all deserve Hell. They further debate whether Christ's atonement was for all people in potentiality, or was it limited to a particular redemption for the Elect?

Those are a few glaring inconsistencies with the Calvinistic system. Their attempt at explanation or defense too often requires a Biblical gymnast in reason.

Chapter 6: The Choice for Election

When the words *elect, election, choice,* or *chosen* are aligned, a pattern and category that appears. Some usage is for service or God's purposes; other usages are for a title of the Believer—whether man or angel. Finally, there is the usage concerning one's salvation, yet not to Salvation. Obviously, God makes choices Whose purposes and wisdom is known only to Him. There are a few verses that appear to claim Man's salvation is already decided, until one closely evaluated the language further. God chose the Messianic line to come through Noah, Shem, Abraham, Isaac, Jacob, Judah, and David. He chose Israel above other Nations, or Jesus above all others or the Church to be in Jesus above Israel for the New Testament Gospel. Each individual—whether from the Old or New Testament (except Jesus)—had to accept positively and respond to the Gospel without force or compulsion.

Before considering the categories or usages, a person should consider some basic definitions. Most of the definitions will be from the Calvinist, though the Arminian or Biblicist would not reject all of these explanations. The words *elect,* or *election* was used twenty-six times in the Bible, while the word *chosen* was used one hundred twenty-one times. Considering the definitions or explanations is important. There are always different meanings in different contexts! It is also important to note those explanations were most often based on assumptions or conjecture.

Strong defines *elect* in the Old Testament from the word *bachiyr* meaning "to choose, select, chosen one, elect" (Strong, 977). It is most often directed to Israel as God's preferred possession, as a title for which He uses.

Joseph Thayer also defines *elect* or *election* in the following manner:

> In the New Testament, the word *"eklektos,"* means "to obtain salvation through Christ...hence Christians are called the chosen or elect of God.those who have become true partakers of the Christian salvation are contrasted with '*Klātoi,*' those who have been invited but have not shown themselves fitted to obtain it...the choice ones...
>
> b). The Messiah is called preeminently '*Eklektos toû Theou*,' as appointed by God to the most exalted office conceivable...
>
> c). Angels are called *Eklektoi*, as those whom God has chosen out from other created beings...as His highest Ministers in governing the Universe.
>
> 2. Choice, select, the best of its kind or class. (Thayer, 197)
>
> *Eklogā.* a). the act of picking out, choosing. Used of the act of God's free will before the foundation of the world He decreed His blessings to certain persons; particularly that by which he determined to bless certain persons through Christ...according to an election which is due to grace. (Ibid.)

Strong referred to election as "An Eternal act of God in His sovereign pleasure— upon no foreseen merit in them, He chooses certain out of the number of sinful men to be the recipients of the special grace of His spirit, and so be made voluntary partakers or Christ's salvation" (Thayer, 785).

Clarke, in a slightly different manner, defined Election: "unlikely *(1 Timothy 2:14 And Adam was not deceived, but the woman being deceived was in the transgression.)* God draws lines among men by His determinative will…and marks a certain part of mankind to whom the gift shall be available. Old Testament usage for selection for service or to accomplish certain purposes of God not for own benefit" (Ibid., 392).

The Elect of the New Testament, like that of the Old Testament are chosen and called to use for the good of other men. The non-elect in God's own time may become elect. Jewish error stated: "election meant favoritism…It grew up as a fruit of the legalism and exclusiveness that followed the Exile (Romans 9-11)" (Ibid., 393). Clarke went further to state: "The argument of Paul in these famous chapters, was not intended for the establishing a doctrine of Election: the argument was intended to release the doctrine of Election from the bondage of exclusiveness and spiritual pride, and presented as a doctrine of Divine Freedom, fulfilling the purpose of Divine Love" (Ibid., 394).

It also bears noting, Koehler, the Lutheran Theologian, in his attempt to seek a biblical and balanced view of election, without eliminating human will or responsibility, remarks at length:

46

"Relation of the election of grace to the work of grace." – The work of the Holy Ghost, by which we are brought to Christ to salvation, is the fulfillment and execution of the election of grace. Hence, there is so intimate a connection between the two that an error in the one will result in an error in the other. Synergists teach that man contributes something toward his conversion; hence they teach that men are elected in view of this "something" they would contribute. Calvinism teaches that many are foreordained to everlasting death; hence, they teach that the Holy Ghost does not intend to save all men. He who correctly understands and believes as is confessed in Luther's explanation of the Third Article of the Apostles' Creed, will have no difficulty in understanding and believing that, what the Holy Ghost does to bring us to Christ and through faith to heaven, God has purposed and resolved to do for us from eternity.

"This doctrine is the doctrine of the Third Article plus the idea of eternity; in other words, it is the eternal purpose and plan of God to do for the individual what, according to the Third Article, He actually does for him during his lifetime to bring him heaven." (Fritschel, 1940) (Koehler, 187-188)

False teachings on election – Calvinism teaches: "By the decrees of God, for the manifestation of His glory, some men and angles are predestined unto everlasting life, and others foreordained to everlasting death" (Westminster Confession); (cf., Schaff, 3608); (cf., *Triglot*, Introd. No. 225. 226). The Bible knows nothing of predestination unto eternal death. On the contrary, it teaches that God would that all men were saved, and that Mankind alone is at fault if he is lost. (Koehler, 188)

1 Timothy 2:4 Who will have all men to be saved, and to come unto the knowledge of the truth.

Matthew 23:37 O Jerusalem, Jerusalem, thou that killest the prophets, and stonest them which are sent unto thee, how often would I have gathered thy children together, even as a hen gathereth her chickens under her wings, and ye would not!

Hosea 13:9 O Israel, thou hast destroyed thyself; but in me is thine help.

Synergism, while upholding the universality of God's grace and Christ's redemption, teaches that there must be something in Man that influenced and determined God to elect just him and not another. (Cf., *Triglot*, Introd., No. 224). Even the expression that men are elected "in the view faith" makes sense only if there is an element of human merit in faith, but the Bible excludes every merit or worthiness in man as a cause of his election. (Ibid., 188)

2 Timothy 1:9 Who hath saved us, and called us with an holy calling, not according to our works, but according to his own purpose and grace, which was given us in Christ Jesus before the world began,

1 Corinthians 11:6 For if the woman be not covered, let her also be shorn: but if it be a shame for a woman to be shorn or shaven, let her be covered.

Human reason cannot harmonize the two doctrines of the Bible, that God by grace for Christ's sake will have all men to be saved, and that God by grace for Christ's sake elected few to be saved; neither must men try to harmonize them. We can only restate what God has revealed to us in His Word, and we must not begin to guess what He has reserved in His hidden wisdom concerning this mystery. God has not revealed to us all He knows, all He did and intends to do for our salvation, nor His reasons for His acts. However, God did reveal as much as He wants us to know and as much as we need to know regarding salvation through Christ. He does not satisfy our curiosity as to His secret counsels. (Ibid.)

Hence, a person can say with Paul in Romans 11:33, *O the depth of the riches both of the wisdom and knowledge of God! how unsearchable are his judgments, and his ways past finding out!*

Koehler did well to identify human reason does not have all the answers or understanding. We do not have a license of conjecture or inference when the Scripture is silent, or our definition contradicts revealed Scripture as often as synergists or Calvinists do. It also must be noted for those holding to Reformed Theology, that infant baptism does not seal one's election either. Symbolism can never replace substance any more than conjectures can replace facts.

Troublesome Verses And Balanced Explanations

Below is a list of a few verses that Calvinists claim as some of their proof text. There are others, but they are redundant or of a similar category. Remember, no one denies that God makes choices uninfluenced by man. No one denies that God elects—chooses people or nations for His purpose or plans. He even does so in accordance with His omniscience, of which His foreknowledge is an extension. It must also be noted, God's foreknowledge is the ability to be just that— foreknowledge. It is not equivalent or subordinate to a decree of predestination, or election, but the reverse is true. God decrees Predestination or elects by His knowledge. No one can pretend to know God's mind or knowledge.

> *Romans 11:33-34, O the depth of the riches both of the wisdom and knowledge of God! how unsearchable are his judgments, and his ways past finding out! For who hath known the mind of the Lord? Or who hath been his counsellor?*

So again one sees the applied usage of *elect, election, choose,* or *chosen* are categories and contexts where those words were mentioned. For instance, Ephesians 1:4 tells the Believers: *"He hath chosen us in Him before the foundation of the World..."* The context is the spiritual blessings one has in Christ in heavenly places.

The second context asks for, or for what has a person been chosen? That is easy to answer! The Believer in this Era or Dispensation of Grace (as opposed to the Old Testament in Israel) was chosen (elected) 1.) to be in Christ; 2.) Holy; 3.) without blame; and 4.) in love. God's choosing was His purpose for the New Testament believer, which He determined before Creation. That is not Salvation, but its benefits. Unfortunately, the Calvinist supplants context, syntax, and pretext to support their prejudice. A Biblicist cannot.

Consider a few more verses viewed from the biblical interpretive style. That premise helps one discern all mankind have a genuine opportunity to respond to the revelation they are given. All mankind also have an influence and call by the Holy Spirit along the road of life. One can also perceive God foreknows who would or would not accept His gracious offer; and that God, in His infinite grace is not obligated to call or work with men or a person indefinitely.

> *Isaiah 42:1 Behold my servant, whom I uphold; mine elect, in whom my soul delighteth; I have put my spirit upon him: he shall bring forth judgment to the Gentiles.*

The term *elect* (*bachiyr*) is used in reference to God's chosen person, the Messiah, to be Israel's Deliverer as well as that of the Gentiles. Obviously, God is not electing Jesus to be saved; rather it is a title.

Another such use is found in 2 Peter 1:10. Peter admonishes the Believer to "make sure" their calling and election. If that was a reference to Salvation, how can there be any hope of "the perseverance of the saints?"

The word *sure* means "to make firm, establish, confirm," and *make sure*: 'to make good the promises by the event, i.e., to fulfill them'" (Thayer's and Smith's Bible Dictionary, 99).

It is in that latter sense like Paul that Peter is using the idea making sure one's calling and election in the context is to *fulfill* or *make good on the promises* of their election and calling. That clearly referred to one's responsible behavior in Salvation and their service and blessing or purpose. It is not as the commentator and Calvinist Albert Barnes, expounded: "…they were to act as to make it certain to themselves that they had been chosen, and were truly called into the Kingdom of God (Barnes, 224).

In other words, according to the Calvinist mindset, some form of works proves grace, election, regeneration, predestination, and other related ideas. That is quite a contradiction to that system of philosophical logic. It is also quite a quagmire of theology.

It is good to consider what one noted commentator observed about election in defining the meaning and application: "While Christ's death was sufficient for all men, and is effective in the case of the elect, yet men are treated as responsible, being capable of the will and power to choose" (Vine, 362).

The final verse to consider is 2 Thessalonians 2:13.

2 Thessalonians 2:13 But we are bound to give thanks alway to God for you, brethren beloved of the Lord, because God hath from the beginning chosen you to salvation through sanctification of the Spirit and belief of the truth:

That passage is one of the charter verses for Calvinists, which by appearance seems one is chosen unto Salvation; however when Scripture is compared and defined by Scripture, a person can get a better understanding of how God applied the meaning. First, there are Scriptures which directly infer or state God's heart for the salvation of all humanity. In 1 Timothy 2:4, Paul says that *"God would have all men to be saved..."* and Peter declared in 2 Peter 3:9, that *"God is not willing that any should perish but that all should come to repentance."* God repeatedly called Israel His chosen. In 1 Timothy 4:10, Christ was declared to be the *"Saviour of all men, specially of those that believe."* Just from those Scriptures, as well as several others, one can conclude simply being *chosen to* or *for* Salvation does not equivocate or produce Salvation. First Timothy 4:10 further expounded there must be genuine belief/faith. In the syntax of the verse, Christ also chooses His Father's plan. The Holy Spirit's role is setting one apart, but people still must make a choice of their own volition to believe.

The context of 2 Thessalonians 2:13 refers to The Great Tribulation. The greater mass of people will freely be willing to choose their unrighteousness and damnation rather than receive the "love of truth" (Verse 10) or "believe not the truth" (Verse 12). Salvation is a choice by a free moral agent, aided or convicted by the Holy Spirit to believe. That was God's plan and choice from Eternity Past—that man could and would be saved. That choice was also God's master plan for grace.

So God's election (or choosing) is for His eternal purpose and service for the *whosoever will*. Therefore they are *The Chosen Ones* or *Elect Ones* as a <u>title</u>, and the process is His <u>method</u>.

Below is a list of the usage of the word *elect*, *election*, or *chose/chosen* regarding one's position, purpose, title, or uses.

Title=Reference to person.

Purpose=Reference to God's purpose in salvation.

Method=Reference to God's method of choice.

THE ELECT		
TITLE	**PURPOSE**	**METHOD**
Isaiah 42:1	Isaiah 42:1	
Isaiah 45:4	Isaiah 45:4	
Isaiah 65:9	Isaiah 65:9	
Isaiah 65:22	Isaiah 65:22	
Matthew 24:22		
Matthew 24:24		
Matthew 24:31		
Mark 13:20		
Mark 13:22		

TITLE	PURPOSE	METHOD
Mark 13:27		
Luke 18:7		
Romans 8:33		
Colossians 3:12		
1 Timothy 5:21		
2 Timothy 2:10		
Titus 1:1	Titus 1:1	
1 Peter 1:2		1 Peter 1:2
1 Peter 2:6	1 Peter 2:6	
	2 John 1:1	
2 John 1:13		
	Romans 9:11	
	Romans 11:5	
	Romans 11:7	
	Romans 11:28	
	1 Thess. 1:4	
	2 Peter 1:10	

THE CHOSEN		
TITLE	PURPOSE	METHOD
	Number 16:5	Number 16:5
	Deut. 7:6	
	Deut.14:2	
	Deut. 18:5	
	Joshua 24:22	
		Judges 10:14
	Judges 20:34	Judges 20:34
		1 Samuel 8:18
	1 Samuel 10:24	1 Samuel 10:24
	1 Samuel 12:13	1 Samuel 12:13
	1 Kings 3:8	
	1 Kings 8:44	
		1 Kings 11:13
	1 Kings 11:32	1 Kings 11:32
	1 Chron. 15:2	
1 Chron. 16:13	1 Chron. 16:13	
	1 Chron. 28:6	
	Psalm 33:12	Psalm 33:12
Psalm 89:3	Psalm 89:3	Psalm 89:3
	Isaiah 58:6	
Isaiah 65:15		

TITLE	PURPOSE	METHOD
Daniel 11:15		
	Haggai 2:23	
	Psalm 89:19	
Psalm 105:6		
Psalm 106:23	Psalm 106:23	
	Isaiah 41:8	Isaiah 41:8
	Isaiah 41:9	Isaiah 41:9
	Isaiah 43:10	Isaiah 43:10
Isaiah 43:20		
		Isaiah 44:1
		Isaiah 44:2
		Zechariah 3:2
	Matthew 12:18	
		Matthew 20:16
		Matthew 22:14
Mark 13:20		
Luke 23:35		
	John 6:70	
	John 13:18	
	John 15:16	
	John 15:19	
	Acts 1:2	Acts 1:2

TITLE	PURPOSE	METHOD
	Acts 22:14	
	Romans 16:13	
	1Cor. 1:27	
	1Cor. 1:28	
	Ephesians 1:4	
		2 Thess. 2:13
	James 2:5	
	1 Peter 2:4	
1 Peter 2:9	1 Peter 2:9	
		Revelation 17:14

Chapter 7: The Calvinist's Dilemmas

This section will begin looking at those beliefs in the Calvinist's system that defy or even outright contradict Scripture. One might even ask why or how can that be? Surely these men are very intelligent men who normally are great defenders of the Scriptures or Salvation by grace through faith. While that may be true, this comment made by Edmond S. Morgan in his work *The Puritan Dilemma* helps to put this idea into context.

> The Puritans tried always to rest their religious principles, like their social, political, legal and moral ones on the Bible, the infallible guidebook for establishing a kingdom of God on earth. But the Bible, while it spoke with unquestioned authority, said different things to different men. To some people, it seemed to prescribe Presbyterianism. To others, Congregationalism; and to a different congregation, it said different things about baptism, or sanctification or communion. (80-81)

During the Reformation, the Reformers initiated persecution toward anyone not aligned with their specific beliefs. The English Non-Calvinist Anglicans under Bishop Laud persecuted Calvinists like the Puritans. After the Synod of Dort, the Calvinists persecuted and harangued all non-Calvinists. With great delight, all of them severely persecuted those considered Anabaptists. All of those men were capable but wrong. They were on the wrong side of history, and as yet unpurged from Romanistic doctrines, thinking, or behavior. "The entire Christian world was engaged in persecution. The Baptists, in all lands, both Protestant and Roman Catholic, were cruelly persecuted by imprisonment, exile, torture, fire, and sword. The Baptists were martyred by the thousands (Christian, 101).

For instance, the majority of Reformers believed in the third through a fifth-century error of infant baptism, which was closely associated with pagan lustration (a ritual or ceremonial cleansing). Thomas Armitage, when quoting Bunsen, wrote regarding pagan lustration that it was an ancient practice with its main features

> 'brought about principally by the Africans of the third century, and completed by Augustine, these natural elements have been, in the course of nearly fifteen centuries, most tragically decomposed, and nothing is now remaining elsewhere but ruins. In the East, people adhere to immersion, although this symbol of a man voluntarily and consciously making a vow of the sacrifice of self, lost all meaning in the immersion of a new-born babe.' (Armitage, 186-187)

He further refuted that with Neander's account on the topic, who stated, "'About the middle of the third century, this theory was already generally admitted into the North African Church. The only question that remained was whether the child ought to be baptized immediately after its birth, or not till eight days after, as in the case of the rite of circumcision.'"(Ibid., 186-187).

The Reformers saw infant baptism as a symbol of New Testament circumcision or sealing of salvation, even though New Testament circumcision was that of the *heart*—of one's free choice of salvation.

60

Romans 2:28-29, For he is not a Jew, which is one outwardly; neither is that circumcision, which is outward in the flesh: But he is a Jew, which is one inwardly; and circumcision is that of the heart, in the spirit, and not in the letter; whose praise is not of men, but of God.

Colossians 2:11, In whom also ye are circumcised with the circumcision made without hands, in putting off the body of the sins of the flesh by the circumcision of Christ:

When Martin Luther was younger, it was said he rejected sprinkling for baptism, but later under Zwingli's and Calvin's pressure, reasserted pouring or sprinkling. He would even suggest a reason for infant baptism could be found in his query whether a child could choose Christ in the womb. In fact, the error of infant baptism contradicted their views of Grace

Martin Luther did not differ substantially from the view expressed by the Roman Catholic Church in the form of baptism. The act of baptism was not an item of controversy at that time, for the Reformers either preferred immersion, as Luther, or held the act to be a matter of indifference, as Calvin. Luther at first followed the practice of dipping the Baptists of Bohemia, for in the early days of the Reformation he leaned heavily on the old evangelicals. [Enders, Luthers Briefwechsel. II. 345, Nr. 280] (Christian, 107)

Luther, undoubtedly under the influence of the Anabaptist, at least initially practiced the immersion even of infants. Christian made note that when he stated:

"It is doubtless true that Luther began by dipping infants. That he taught immersion, there can be no doubt. In his celebrated sermon on Baptism, date 1518, he says, "...the child or anyone who is to be baptized, be completely sunk down into the water..." (Christian, 107-108).

The point one needs to understand here is if the Reformers, specifically Calvinists, are wrong in those beliefs then and now, it is not too difficult to conclude certain other aspects of their beliefs are still wrong. Just believing in "believers' baptism" by immersion does not correct that wrong either, nor does a belief in Pre-millennialism.

Linguistic Contortionism

One of the areas of disappointment is the twisting of normal Scriptural meanings. That problem might be likened to Scriptural contortionism. Perhaps the best example is what is often done with the passage from John 3:16.

John 3:16, For God so loved the world, that he gave his only begotten Son, that whosoever believeth in him should not perish, but have everlasting life.

It is there that one sees the effect of prejudicial deductive interpreting rather than objective inductive translation and interpretation. Here we learn that *all* does not mean *all mankind* or the word *world* mean *the world of all men;* nor does the word *whosoever* mean *anybody.* It only applies to the category of *the predestined elect.*

That translation feat of course only conveniently applies here or wherever Scripture contradicts their view. So they change the normal interpretation for the rare. The stronger Calvinist's strawmen are erected to justify the altered rules of the normal sensible interpretation or translation.

Such rationalism or sophistry questions are posed like: "Does *all* and *world* mean the rocks, planets, and trees?" It then is noted the word for *world* is *Kosmos* and not *Aion* (Age, era, world). As Strong pointed out, the normal understanding of *world* besides the planet is "The inhabitants of men, the human family...the ungodly multitude, the whole mass of men alienated from God, and therefore hostile to the cause of Christ" (386).

Now, where does *Kosmos* (*world*) mean only the selected chosen ones of the world? In fact, quite the opposite! So when one comes to the word *whosoever,* it can only contextually refer to the possibility of anyone of mankind. One can see *whosoever* is the word *pas.* In the normal majority use, it means "all, every, all men, everyone, the whole, every man, what or whosoever." (*Strong's Exhaustive Concordance: King James Version,* 1995)

Individually, "the aforementioned is the vast majority usage and understanding; however, it can on occasion mean "collectively" some of all types. "It is that occasional irregular meaning that the Calvinist prefers because it lines up with their prejudicial deductive interpretation.

Their problem is that *world* still means all mankind, and those *whosoever* must also be a broad potential group and not the irregular meaning (*Hebrew select*). To demonstrate their ability to argue their point, the Calvinist employs mockery or strawmen arguments.

Notice the comments of the great preacher and Calvinist C.H. Spurgeon:

> "The whole world has gone after him" Did all the world go after Christ" "then went all Judea, and were baptized of him in Jordan." Was all Judea, or all Jerusalem, baptized in Jordan? "Ye are of God, little children" and the whole world lieth in the wicked one." Does *the whole world* there mean everybody? The words *world* and *all* are used in some seven or eight different meanings in Scripture, and rarely did the word *all* mean all persons, taken individually. The words were generally used to signify Christ redeemed some of all sorts—some Jews, some Gentiles, some rich, some poor—and had not restricted His redemption to either Jew or Gentile. (C.H. Spurgeon, from a sermon on "Particular Redemption")

From Spurgeon's comments, one sees from where the Calvinist is coming. Simply put, *all* or *world,* means *all*—whether symbolically or expressively—as an overstatement and not merely some from all groupings. Spurgeon's view, like all Calvinists, was based on his own preconceived notion. He was also wrong about Eschatology and admitted to his lack of study in that area. He simply adheres to the Reformed Covenant Theology and teaching of his time. Perhaps as one person stated, that Calvin was wrong about Salvation and Spurgeon was wrong about Calvin.

Limited or Unlimited Atoning Work at Calvary

This area of the discussion is perhaps one of the more obvious differences between a Biblicist and a Calvinist. Under the philosophical deductive system of the Calvinist's idea of *Limited Atonement* is made to look logical if one agrees to two things. First, one must agree to the Calvinistic belief that total depravity means an absolute inability to believe under any circumstance. Second, the preselected are regenerated (quickened) perhaps years in advance, awaiting their flame to be fanned, so they will think they are actually doing the choosing.

Of course, that idea leads them to the unique view of *unconditional election*. That concept is the deduction of the Calvinist's view of the *decree of predestination* of the select persons to salvation over anyone else. It seems therefore only logical that Christ's atoning work need only apply to or be limited to those elected.

After all, of what value is an atonement that is unapproachable or beneficial for the mass of elect humanity.

As man cannot prepare himself to this work, nor produce it, so he cannot cooperate with God in the first production of it. We are no more co-workers with God in the first regeneration, then we were joint purchasers with Christ in redemption. The conversion of the will to God is a voluntary act; but the regeneration of the will, or the planting new habits in the will, whereby it is enabled to turn to God, is without any concurrence of the will. ...for either that act of grace is voluntary or involuntary...since the tone of the will is changed, then the creature concurs in the act: for the act of believing and repenting is the act of the creature: it is not God that repents and believes in us, but we repent and believe by virtue of that power which God hath given us. In the first act, therefore, there is a concurrence of the creature; otherwise, the creature could not be said to repent and believe, but something in the creature, without or against the will of the creature **but in the first power of believing and repenting, God is the sole agent**...The state wherein man is at his first renewal, excludes any co-working with God. (Charnock, 203-204)

So the Sinner, according to the Calvinist concept of Grace, must be brought first to the new life (regeneration), so he can repent of his already granted salvation. This concept is a type of double regeneration.

The Calvinist's glaring problem, however, is that this view is unscriptural. The only limit here is the Calvinist's view of God's sovereign, omnipotent ability, and correct interpretive exegesis. Consider only a few of the following Scriptures as examples.

1 John 2:2 And he is the propitiation for our sins: and not for ours only, but also for the sins of the whole world.

Hebrews 2:9 But we see Jesus, who was made a little lower than the angels for the suffering of death, crowned with glory and honour; that he by the grace of God should taste death for every man.

1 Timothy 4:10 For therefore we both labour and suffer reproach, because we trust in the living God, who is the Saviour of all men, specially of those that believe.

1 Timothy 2:6 Who gave himself a ransom for all, to be testified in due time.

2 Corinthians 5:14 For the love of Christ constraineth us; because we thus judge, that if one died for all, then were all dead:

The Calvinist must misappropriate or manipulate these scriptures. He must reinterpret the obvious out of context. In First Timothy, the Believer must pray for *all* men whom for Christ died and not just an elect.

1 Timothy 2:1 I exhort therefore, that, first of all, supplications, prayers, intercessions, and giving of thanks, be made for all men;

This dishonest exegesis is done in order to justify a theory blatantly extra or unscriptural. The Calvinist does this out of a confusion of universal provision and opportunity with universal salvation (the heart of modernism). Besides, in their system, *all* can only mean the elect sinners are the saved ones. This is known in philosophy as *circular reasoning* (A=B because B=A).

Honest Calvinists like Dabney recognize this: In 2 Cor. V:15 we make *the all* for whom Christ died, mean only *the all* who live unto Him—i.e. the elect—it would seem to be implies that of those elect for

67

whom Christ died, only part will live to Christ" To get around the universal aspects of the passage, Custance admits that Christ really died for all men, but then claims that Christ died "not for men's sinful actions but for man's sinful condition. (Vance, 445)

So to defuse the unscriptural label of a "Limited Atonement," the Calvinist of more modern times have referred to a "Particular Redemption." That concept somewhat admits to a universal atonement. So the non-elect stand condemned, and only the Elect, in particular, can be redeemed.

Regardless of the terminology one chooses to use, in reality, that concept is still a limitation of offer and application. So long as the predestined elect only benefit, and a hopeless humanity does not, then according to a Calvinist's view, the words can be tweaked. It is nonetheless unbiblical, and every attempt to redefine *all* as *not all* or only a few select equals, *all* is unsupportive. All the flabbergasted conclude or suggest this is the definition of man's depravity, grace, regeneration, predestination, or election as the only viable explanations. Furthermore, that anyone saved, (if one can really know as a Calvinist) must be satisfied with those explanations of God's goodness and love, as well as the hopelessness of the mass of lost humanity.

Depravity or Denial: The Dilemma of the Human Will

Many years ago at my ordination, I was asked to comment on the depravity of man. There were those pastors on the council who were strong Calvinists and those who were not. My answer satisfied or dissatisfied

68

both parties. In referencing man's depravity, I declared that man's depravity was categorically different from Satan's and the demonic host. Man's depravity was a perversion or bent of his moral nature, in which his sin ultimately wins out. That realization is important also in thwarting the heretical teaching of Thomas Aquinas. He believed one could ascend the mind to become sinless.

> Aquinas held that man had revolted against God and thus was fallen, but Aquinas had an incomplete view of the Fall. He thought that the Fall did not affect man as a whole but only in part. In his view, the will was fallen or corrupted, but the intellect was not affected. Thus people could rely on their own human wisdom, and this meant that people were free to mix the teachings of the Bible with the teachings of the non-Christian philosophers. *(*Schaeffer, 51-52*)*

Though some would deny this point, Aquinas was a counter-Reformation Theologian.

Satan's depravity, however, was an *inversion.* His original nature was now completely evil and never capable of guilt, conviction, noble actions, or any level of good.

"So Satan is darkness, and in him is no light at all; 'there is no truth in him'" (Trench, 95).

> *John 8:44 Ye are of your father the devil, and the lusts of your father ye will do. He was a murderer from the beginning, and abode not in the truth, because there is no truth in him. When he speaketh a lie, he*

speaketh of his own: for he is a liar, and the father of it.

"Man is in a middle position; he retains the truth in unrighteousness" (Ibid).

Romans 1:18 For the wrath of God is revealed from heaven against all ungodliness and unrighteousness of men, who hold the truth in unrighteousness;

"Light and darkness in him are struggling, but whichever may predominate. Thus, redemption is possible for man, for his will is only perverted; but Satan's is inverted. He has said what no man could ever fully say, or at least act on to the full: 'Evil, be thou my good;' and therefore, so far as we can see, a redemption and restoration are impossible for him" (Ibid).

His mind and operation are eternally selfish evil. That understanding is the great theological distinction between Man and the Devils' sin nature that is not really made by Calvinists. They might agree that the fallen angels are fixed in their evil but avoid that distinction with the Man, or carry that thought and distinction to its logical conclusion. For the Calvinist sins effect upon man's spiritual, moral nature, mind, body, spirit, emotion or will is essentially the same as Satan's.

Angelic beings, however, are categorically different creatures than humans. Their original privileges, power, intellectual and structure is different from humans. Their test and fall into sin bore some similarity but was also uniquely different. That is why there is no grace offer, no redemption, no faith and repentance response, no forgiveness, and no regeneration. They, no matter the influences upon them, can never choose God and righteousness; but man does.

The million-dollar question is How? How does the sinfully depraved and spiritually dead man choose as an act of his sinful will, God's salvation? For the Calvinist man cannot and will not ever unless God first regenerates his mind and spirit.

> Regeneration is that act of God by which the governing disposition of the soul is made holy, and by which, through the truth as a means, the first holy exercise of this disposition is secured.

> Regeneration or the new birth is the divine side of that change of heart which, viewed from the human side, we call conversion. It is God's turning the soul to himself, - conversion being the soul's turning itself to God, of which God's turning it is both the accompaniment and cause. It will be observed from the above definition, that there are two aspects of regeneration, in the first of which the soul is passive, in the second of which the soul is active. God changes the governing disposition, - in this change the soul is simply acted upon. God secures the initial exercise of this disposition in view of the truth. In this change, the soul itself acts. These two parts of God's operation are simultaneous. At the same moment that He makes the soul sensitive, He pours in the light of His truth

and ***induces*** the exercise of the holy disposition has imparted. (Strong, 809)

Furthermore, only those preselected (elect) shall respond. That is how the Calvinist attempts to escape the box they have placed themselves in by not distinguishing the effects of human vs. satanic depravity and the will.

Such a notion is blatantly unscriptural and lays at the core question. Is salvation of man chosen for him by God alone in every aspect, or does enabled man freely choose? Chosen or choice? Well, has the Savior pointed out that "without me ye can do nothing"?

John 15:5   I am the vine, ye are the branches: He that abideth in me, and I in him, the same bringeth forth much fruit: for without me ye can do nothing.

And..

Mark 10:27   And Jesus looking upon them saith, With men it is impossible, but not with God: for with God all things are possible.

Notice some of the Scriptural admonitions for Man to choose from God's Word:

John 4:14   But whosoever drinketh of the water that I shall give him shall never thirst; but the water that I shall give him shall be in him a well of water springing up into everlasting life.

Deuteronomy 30:19   I call heaven and earth to record this day against you, that I have set before you life and death, blessing and cursing: therefore choose life, that both thou and thy seed may live:

Mark 10:21 Then Jesus beholding him loved him, and said unto him, One thing thou lackest: go thy way, sell whatsoever thou hast, and give to the poor, and thou shalt have treasure in heaven: and come, take up the cross, and follow me.

Acts 2:38 Then Peter said unto them, Repent, and be baptized every one of you in the name of Jesus Christ for the remission of sins, and ye shall receive the gift of the Holy Ghost.

Acts 13:38-43 Be it known unto you therefore, men and brethren, that through this man is preached unto you the forgiveness of sins: And by him all that believe are justified from all things, from which ye could not be justified by the law of Moses. Beware therefore, lest that come upon you, which is spoken of in the prophets; Behold, ye despisers, and wonder, and perish: for I work a work in your days, a work which ye shall in no wise believe, though a man declare it unto you. And when the Jews were gone out of the synagogue, the Gentiles besought that these words might be preached to them the next sabbath. Now when the congregation was broken up, many of the Jews and religious proselytes followed Paul and Barnabas: who, speaking to them, persuaded them to continue in the grace of God.

Acts 14:15 And saying, Sirs, why do ye these things? We also are men of like passions with you, and preach unto you that ye should turn from these vanities unto the living God, which made heaven, and earth, and the sea, and all things that are therein:

Acts 17:32-34 And when they heard of the resurrection of the dead, some mocked: and others said, We will hear thee again of this matter. So Paul departed from among them. Howbeit certain men clave unto him, and believed: among the which was Dionysius the Areopagite, and a woman named Damaris, and others with them.

Acts 19:17-18 And this was known to all the Jews and Greeks also dwelling at Ephesus; and fear fell on them all, and the name of the Lord Jesus was magnified. And many that believed came, and confessed, and shewed their deeds.

It is already known that God has chosen the preaching of the Cross to save sinners, and that the Word of God divides the person as a sword, and that it is the cause of the Believer's faith.

1 Corinthians 1:17-18 For Christ sent me not to baptize, but to preach the gospel: not with wisdom of words, lest the cross of Christ should be made of none effect. For the preaching of the cross is to them that perish foolishness; but unto us which are saved it is the power of God.

Hebrews 4:12 For the word of God is quick, and powerful, and sharper than any twoedged sword, piercing even to the dividing asunder of soul and spirit, and of the joints and marrow, and is a discerner of the thoughts and intents of the heart.

Additionally, one knows the Holy Spirit, while given as a guide to the Believer is also the convicting Agent of sin, righteousness, and judgment upon the world of mankind.

John 16:8 And when he is come, he will reprove the world of sin, and of righteousness, and of judgment:

So no person in this Age of Grace will truly be without excuse. The question before us is whether our Lord really meant the world of all mankind would experience a direct reprove by the Holy Spirit or just a few elect? Is the Holy Spirit truly the agent to which Christ was referring when He declared in John 12:32, *"And I, if I be lifted up from the earth, will draw all men unto me."*

Does not *all* mean *all*? All do not have to respond or choose even if the crucified Christ is humanity's focal point. History and Scripture validate that truth.

So the Holy Spirit's message and drawing, coupled with the living power of God's Word, brings sinners to the focus of the cross—where they must choose. While the event of Salvation is singular, the process to come often takes a series of yielded choices to God's Call. Let the Old Testament be the example of Grace that no regeneration took place before belief. Whether it was Noah, Abraham, Isaac, Jacob, Moses, or others—they all had to personally choose God of their volition, without first being regenerated. That choice must also be so under the New Testament Grace if one properly defines the work of Grace.

As previously stated, race or election does not render man a puppet, robot, or passive acquirer. Consider what Wayne Grudem commented about the human will:

> It is better to affirm that God causes all things that happen, but that he does so in such a way that he somehow upholds our ability to make willing, responsible choices, choices that have real and eternal results, and for which we are held accountable. Exactly how God combines his providential control with our willing and significant choices, Scripture does not explain to us. But rather than deny one aspect or the other (simply because we cannot explain how both can be true), we should accept both in an attempt to be faithful to the teaching of all Scripture. (321-322)

Another false notion and logical conclusion of man's will being totally subverted under the Calvinist's understanding of grace, election, predestination, and one's will is the dilemma caused after salvation. If Calvinists are correct, then why are some men spiritual giants, and some mediocre or carnal? Have they also been chosen to that condition? Is their will supplanted or completely freed from depravity?

The Calvinist will staunchly object. They will cry "Foul!" because the Holy Spirit can conquer Man's sin nature in the New Man.

> *2 Corinthians 5:17 Therefore if any man be in Christ, he is a new creature: old things are passed away; behold, all things are become new.*

Scriptures declare one is now a *New Creature*. People can now be free to yield to sin or Christ because of the Holy Spirit.

> *Romans 6:8-14 Now if we be dead with Christ, we believe that we shall also live with him: Knowing that Christ being raised from the dead dieth no more; death hath no more dominion over him. For in that he died, he died unto sin once: but in that he liveth, he liveth unto God. Likewise reckon ye also yourselves to be dead indeed unto sin, but alive unto God through Jesus Christ our Lord. Let not sin therefore reign in your mortal body, that ye should obey it in the lusts thereof. Neither yield ye your members as instruments of unrighteousness unto sin: but yield yourselves unto God, as those that are alive from the dead, and your members as instruments of righteousness unto God. For sin shall not have dominion over you: for ye are not under the law, but under grace.*

Wait a minute! Is the saved person yielding to Christ of their own volition under the Holy Spirit's influence, or can they resist the Spirit's prompting?! Then why can the fact that he resisted not be true before Salvation? Do the equation. Alternatively, if Salvation was purely a fixed, unwitting regeneration before yielding and calling for Salvation, then so is spiritual growth. God commanded Christians to grow, fight, be perfect, be holy, and more, but under equal logic, the outcome must also be predetermined. Note, the Athenians were commanded by Paul "to repent." In pointing out that contradiction to one younger new Calvinist, he responded, "Then it must be so." That point is a great dilemma for the Calvinist too. How can their equation be imbalanced and their position so unequal?

Lost humanity is invited to Salvation, where he must exercise his will to do so under the Spirit's calling, reproving, and enabling. The Spirit and the Bride are inviting *whosoever will*. That invitation can be seen in some of the following few verses:

> *Revelation 22:17 And the Spirit and the bride say, Come. And let him that heareth say, Come. And let him that is athirst come. And whosoever will, let him take the water of life freely.*

> *Acts 17:30 And the times of this ignorance God winked at; but now commandeth all men every where to repent:*

> *Romans 10:11 For the scripture saith, Whosoever believeth on him shall not be ashamed.*

> *Romans 10:13 For whosoever shall call upon the name of the Lord shall be saved.*

> *Acts 26:20 But shewed first unto them of Damascus, and at Jerusalem, and throughout all the coasts of Judaea, and then to the Gentiles, that they should repent and turn to God, and do works meet for repentance.*

So the clear and simple teaching of Scripture militates against the Calvinist suppositions. In fact, if like Wayne Grudem insisted that man must have a real choice and that God's assertive Providence is in no way diminished, then both concepts are Scriptural and are being worked together by God (Grudem, 323). With Man having a fallen but capable assisted will, he is then capable of real choice of rejecting or accepting God's grace offer. That being so, then the whole concept of the Calvinist's TULIP comes tumbling down like the proverbial house of cards.

Grudem's statement is not Partnership Salvation as Pelagius taught, or independent intellect as Aquinas supposed. It is God being sovereign and working "all things together" at the same time. That concept of Sovereignty is also true in the case of Evil. God does not cause or author Evil, but He does ordain it and uses it for His eternally good purposes or plan.

Genesis 50:20 But as for you, ye thought evil against me; but God meant it unto good, to bring to pass, as it is this day, to save much people alive.

Consider Joseph's comment to his brothers above. He was a clear picture of choices. One choice was sinful and brought to account, and God's providence was overriding to bring about good. Wayne Grudem's insights about God and Pharaoh concerning the following verses provided a helpful view:

> *Exodus 8:15 But when Pharaoh saw that there was respite, he hardened his heart, and hearkened not unto them; as the LORD had said.*

> *Exodus 8:32 And Pharaoh hardened his heart at this time also, neither would he let the people go.*

> *Exodus 9:34 And when Pharaoh saw that the rain and the hail and the thunders*

79

were ceased, he sinned yet more, and hardened his heart, he and his servants.

Exodus 4:21 And the LORD said unto Moses, When thou goest to return into Egypt, see that thou do all those wonders before Pharaoh, which I have put in thine hand: but I will harden his heart, that he shall not let the people go.

Exodus 7:3 And I will harden Pharaoh's heart, and multiply my signs and my wonders in the land of Egypt.

Exodus 8:15 But when Pharaoh saw that there was respite, he hardened his heart, and hearkened not unto them; as the LORD had said.

Some people object to the fact Scripture also says that Pharaoh hardened his heart and that God's act of hardening Pharaoh's heart was only in response to the initial rebellion and hardness of heart that Pharaoh himself exhibited of his own free will. But it should be noted that God's promises that he would harden Pharaoh's heart (Ex. 4:21; 7:3) are made long before Scripture tells us that Pharaoh hardened his own heart (we read of this for the first time in Exodus 8:15). Moreover, our analysis of concurrence given above, in which both divine and human agents can cause the same event, should show us that both factors can be true at the same time: even when Pharaoh hardens his own heart, that is not inconsistent with saying that God is causing Pharaoh to do this and thereby God is hardening the heart of Pharaoh. (Grudem, 323)

That is a sovereign God working ALL things together for good. The point is everything coalesces in God and His plan; sin nature and free, legitimate choice.

Chapter 8: When Grace is No Longer Grace!

Galatians 2:21 I do not frustrate the grace of God: for if righteousness come by the law, then Christ is dead in vain.

When asked "What is Grace and what does it mean?" the average Christian usually responds with what they have heard or what they have been taught. The usual response was that it means a free gift. Alternatively, some people may respond grace is that which has been bestowed (some favor granting or gift) without merit and therefore unearnable, underserved and unrepayable. Grace also is the vehicle by which a Believer is empowered to perform the will and life God has declared.

Chafer defines grace in this way, "The word *favor* is the nearest Biblical synonym for the word grace…Grace is favor and favor is grace…Grace means pure, unrecompensed kindness and favor" (Chaffer, 3-4).

Strong saw it as enforcing the Law! "God is to be regarded, however, not as abrogating the law, but as republishing and enforcing it. (Strong, 547)."

Romans 3:31 Do we then make void the law through faith? God forbid: yea, we establish the law.

Thus, the revelation of grace, while it takes up and includes in itself the revelation of Law, adds something different in kind, namely, the manifestation of the personal love of the Lawgiver. Without Grace, the Law has only a demanding aspect. Only in connection with Grace does it become the perfect law—the law of liberty. (Strong, 547-548)

James 1:25 But whoso looketh into the perfect law of liberty, and continueth therein, he being not a forgetful hearer, but a doer of the work, this man shall be blessed in his deed.

Strong further stated: "In fine, grace is that larger and completer manifestation of the divine nature, of which law constitutes the necessary but preparatory stage" (Ibid., 549).

Another Theologian, Edward Koehler, describes Grace this way: "The word *grace* is sometimes used of a gift, quality, virtue or power which God imparts to man gratuitously. The grace of God by which we are saved is the *favor Dei*, which is that merciful, affectionate disposition, that good will of God towards men, according to which He forgives sins to those who are worthy of eternal death. It is the unmerited love of God toward me" (Koehler, 79).

John 3:16 For God so loved the world, that he gave his only begotten Son, that whosoever believeth in him should not perish, but have everlasting life.

Titus 3:4-5 But after that the kindness and love of God our Saviour toward man appeared, Not by works of righteousness which we have done, but according to his mercy he saved us, by the washing of regeneration, and renewing of the Holy Ghost;

83

"From this concept of grace must be excluded every regard for the merit of man. God's grace is not in the least affected, motivated, or influenced by any worthiness in us; in fact, the slightest injection of man's merit and worthiness utterly destroys the concept of grace" (Koehler, 79).

Finally, Clarke simplified these ideas by stating: "It should be added only that Grace, which is prominent in the Scriptural statements, is love in God regarded as free and unpurchased, coming out of its own accord to bless the undeserving. It stands to all forms and phases of the idea of merit" (Clarke, 102).

Today, God's grace has fallen on hard times in its application and offer. Seemingly, it no longer acts as true grace. We are deluged from modern Evangelicals with a Libertine grace that allows one to be a believer with no standards of holiness or conviction. Of course, the opposite is also true when so many rules are placed upon a believer that they stumble or suffocate. There has always been the battle over *cheap grace*. While that may lead to a Libertine life, it is based on either a formula or a ritualistic Christianity. Sometimes it adds liturgical religiosity to garner grace. Some Evangelical groups, usually engaged in "easy believism." That notion is a faith with no repentance. In fact, that type faith was often expressed through the words of a simple prayer where no life change followed.

Of course, there is the Roman, English and Eastern Catholics as well as some Lutherans who believe in essence that grace is insufficient and must have their organization and works also. That system essentially nullifies Grace. In that context is the belief of the

Calvinist that saving grace for humanity is unobtainable unless a person is the predestined Elect. Yes, humanity benefits for what is referred to as *universal* or *common grace*, where there is the allowance of some good to exist.

Henry Meeter commented on that very concept:

> But how can God love and hate the same persons at the same time? If he hates the wicked, the reprobate, and will punish them for their sins, how can He be said in any sense to love them. But on the infralapsarian viewpoint, God first decided to create human beings. As such they are all conceived as objects of His love. Then God decided to permit the Fall and in His electing love to save some and to pass by others, the non-elect and punish them in His wrath for their sins. On this basis, it is possible for God to love the non-elect as creatures. A parallel instance would be the case of the righteous father whose misdeeds demand his expulsion. But the Calvinist sees everywhere, in the pagan world and among unbelievers, wherever science, art, and culture are brought to higher levels, the working of God's Holy Spirit, fruits which God has brought to pass in spite of the wickedness of the natural heart of man. The Calvinist thankfully accepts these fruits as products of God's grace and claims them for God's Kingdom. (Meeter, 76-78)

It is that rigid belief and limiting of Grace a person cannot willingly exercise true faith without first being regenerated. Anything else is considered to be *works.* There can be no human volition or repentance or response without the controlling influence or **dictation** by the Holy Spirit. In their line of philosophical logic, that was the requirement of God's grace or mercy. This thinking is inconsistent with Grace being unmerited favor— regardless of biblical declarations.

> *Revelation 22:17 And the Spirit and the bride say, Come. And let him that heareth say, Come. And let him that is athirst come. And whosoever will, let him take the water of life freely.*

So when John, in Revelation 22:17 invited the *whosoever will* he really did not invite *all* or *anyone.* No, it was only the *whosoever* of those that have been preselected from Eternity Past to Salvation. The common person now needs training in Greek to re-interpret simple grammar.

That complex idea frustrates the Grace of God to where grace is no longer true grace or mercy. The invitation becomes insincere at best. The Calvinist will immediately object at this point. They respond with a "quite the contrary" argument. For them, since all people are hell-bound and deserve it, anything God does is the demonstration of Grace. In the theoretical arena, that thought would be true. The problem with that thinking is it limits God's nature or demonstration of love, mercy, omniscience, and omnipotence. It presumes to *KNOW* God's plan and purposes, or His mind. This presumption is how the Calvinist *interprets* God's elective grace.

86

Strong, a Classical Calvinist, proves the previous point when he stated:

> The depravity of the human will is such that, without this decree to bestow special divine influences upon some, all, without exception, would have rejected Christ's salvation after it was offered to them; and so all, without exception, must have perished. Election, therefore, may be viewed as a necessary consequence of God's decree to provide an objective redemption, if that redemption is to have any subjective result in human salvation.

> The doctrine of election becomes more acceptable to reason when we remember: first, that God's decree is eternal, and in a certain sense is contemporaneous with man's belief in Christ; secondly that God's decree to create involves the decree of all that in the exercise of man's freedom will follow; thirdly, that God's decree is the decree of him who is all in all, so that our willing and doing is at the same time working with him who decrees our willing and doing. The whole question turns upon the initiative in human salvation: if this belongs to God, then in spite of difficulties we must accept the doctrine of election.

> It is unjust to those who are not included in this purpose of salvation. Answer: Election deals, not simply with creatures, but with sinful, guilty, and condemned creatures.

> That any should be saved, is a matter of pure grace, and those who are not included in this purpose of salvation suffer only the due reward of their deeds. There is, therefore, no injustice in God's election. We may better praise God that he saves any than charging him with injustice because he saves so few. (Strong, 784-785)

One must ask if God is limited to those He supposedly preselected and compelled, or can anyone potentially respond if they are human and enabled by God's Spirit? Is this not the Holy Spirit's ministry? Is it true that mankind as a whole only benefits from God's "common grace," which essentially permits their existence? Titus 2:11 states:

> *Titus 2:11 For the grace of God that bringeth salvation hath appeared to all men,*

So unless we practice deceitful misuse of the words *all men*; then in some manner, God's grace has and is appearing to all men with regards to salvation. That is more than common (universal) grace or a disingenuine offer, or a dual call system. In fact, in verse 12 those who responded to God's grace see it as not only the access to salvation but their teacher of righteousness. God's saving grace then as already seen, has been revealed to all men; and as also seen it has been and can be resisted.

Now under God's grace and foreknowledge, people can find a reason why the Gospel spoken by believers or preachers may not have gone into all the world. God knows who and when concerning exercised

88

faith, as well as the Believer's faithless disobedience to proclaim the Gospel of Grace. That idea is not only a frustration of Grace but a perversion of the working of grace. That is why under the hyper, supra, or *infralapsarian* Calvinist systems, true revivals or missions too often become stunted or nonexistent. Believers become subjective in their faith and rationalistic in their calling and outreach. Simple obedience is not apparently enough for the Believer. That is why personal responsibility for cause and effect can never be removed. When great revivals did occur under Calvinistic men who preached despite their theology, their messages were at times contradictory to their theology. Christians therefore, must always like Ezekiel, see themselves as the watchman.

> *Ezekiel 33:6 But if the watchman see the sword come, and blow not the trumpet, and the people be not warned; if the sword come, and take any person from among them, he is taken away in his iniquity; but his blood will I require at the watchman's hand.*

Perhaps one of History's best illustrations of this mentality was William Carey before the British Baptist Union Mission Council. While defending his belief to bring the Gospel to India, one preacher argued that if God had chosen those pagans to be saved, He would have sent them the Gospel already. After that, Carey responded in effect, "He has. He has chosen me to go." Therein is the balance of God's directive grace and human responsibility. Thus Grace is neither cheapened nor frustrated. It must be free to all or none would respond at all.

Today, Mankind is freed from the constraints of the Law by its fulfillment in Christ.

Matthew 5:17-18 Think not that I am come to destroy the law, or the prophets: I am not come to destroy, but to fulfill. For verily I say unto you, Till heaven and earth pass, one jot or one tittle shall in no wise pass from the law, till all be fulfilled.

Romans 10:4 For Christ is the end of the law for righteousness to every one that believeth.

Adam's sin and his offering as well have been paid at Calvary by Christ alone as God's sin offering.

John 1:29 The next day John seeth Jesus coming unto him, and saith, Behold the Lamb of God, which taketh away the sin of the world.

A sin offering established in Eden was humanity's reminder of better things to come.

Genesis 3:21 Unto Adam also and to his wife did the LORD God make coats of skins, and clothed them.

Genesis 4:4 And Abel, he also brought of the firstlings of his flock and of the fat thereof. And the LORD had respect unto Abel and to his offering:

Leviticus 17:10 And whatsoever man there be of the house of Israel, or of the strangers that sojourn among you, that eateth any manner of blood; I will even set my face against that soul that eateth blood, and will cut him off from among his people.

Hebrews 9:23 It was therefore necessary that the patterns of things in the heavens should be purified with these; but the heavenly things themselves with better sacrifices than these.

Hebrews 12:24 And to Jesus the mediator of the new covenant, and to the blood of sprinkling, that speaketh better things than that of Abel.

Since man's transgression has been paid in full by mankind's potential Redeemer:

Romans 10:4 For Christ is the end of the law for righteousness to every one that believeth.

Galatians 3:13 Christ hath redeemed us from the curse of the law, being made a curse for us: for it is written, Cursed is every one that hangeth on a tree:

Colossians 1:14 In whom we have redemption through his blood, even the forgiveness of sins:

All that remains for mankind is to experience the benefit of redemption and the renewal of regeneration. Justification (righteousness) is legally imparted by only one means, then Salvation is for all who genuinely believe, placing their faith in Christ alone for mercy.

Hebrews 2:4 God also bearing them witness, both with signs and wonders, and with divers miracles, and gifts of the Holy Ghost, according to his own will?

91

John 3:16 For God so loved the world, that he gave his only begotten Son, that whosoever believeth in him should not perish, but have everlasting life.

Galatians 3:11 But that no man is justified by the law in the sight of God, it is evident: for, The just shall live by faith.

Hebrews 11:6 But without faith it is impossible to please him: for he that cometh to God must believe that he is, and that he is a rewarder of them that diligently seek him.

That is why God's grace from beginning to end has always been rich unto all that call upon Him.

Chapter 9: The Calvinist's Calvinism

The Conflict of Scripture

Whether discussing the system of the T.U.L.I.P., the Nature of God, God's partially or unrevealed work in Eternity Past, or the interpretation or application of Scriptures, the Calvinist or Arminian has a conflict with Scripture. When a seldom-used interpretation of Scripture is employed to make one's system stand, there is a problem. When reinterpreting commonly used words such as *all* or *whosoever* by holding up other possible usages as a strawman, there is a conflict of Scriptural integrity.

There is also a Scriptural conflict when one uses exaggerated figures of speech that are comments on Israel, or God's purpose and power are applied to the New Testament saints. Such examples as "Jacob have I loved," and other similar phrases, or the point about Pharaoh's heart, or the vessels of wrath from Romans chapter nine are cited out of context in the attempt to prove their position. Scriptures are assumed from a Reformed–Covenant position rather than from a Dispensational one. Romans nine is a vindication of God's sovereign purposes in the salvation of Gentiles.

Further conflicts of Scripture occur when a person presumes to know the mind or methods of God in Eternity Past concerning Salvation. That conflict occurs when people twist the meanings used for *election, predestination, calling,* or *foreknowledge.* Scriptural myopia can occur when one approaches the Scriptures or words from their own deductive or pre-suppositional position.

The Biblicist cannot do this!

The Conflict with God's Law and His Nature of Justice

The Law(s) of God, which were moral in nature, for Israel were based upon His holiness and justice. Within those laws of justice, three elements were always at work. First, all laws had to be **Equitable**. There could be no partiality or favoritism (respecters of men). Both the noble class and poor were to be equal under the Law. When partly occurred then justice would be fallen in the streets and tyranny would occur.

The second element is **Retribution** (Recompense). If one commits a crime, then one must receive the just sentence under the Law; no more and no less. Mercy could be granted, such as cities of refuge, or the rules of redemption or the substitutionary blood sacrifices for sin. The best demonstration of God's retributive justice, holiness, and love is a Calvary with the capital crime of Sin with the death penalty having to be carried out upon humanities representative.

The third element of God's justices is **Culpability**. God would violate all three elements of His just law and nature of justice. That violation would have cataclysmic circumstances to the Godhead. Obviously, that is a conflict for the Calvinist. Each person, not others, are responsible for their own faults and given true opportunity to believe or repent.

The Conflict of God's Nature of Love

Dave Hunt posed to the Calvinist one simple question, "What Love Is This?" He would cite inconsistencies or inaccuracies with the Calvinist position. Not to appear too much a Platonist, but human love(s), no matter how imperfect under sin's influence, are still a reflection of the Creator's love. Like faith, God is the originator.

So, a love of a family that detests and rejects most of the children and in partiality loves a few of them over the other, evokes the thought "What Love is This?" Furthermore, when it is proclaimed that the parent loves all his children but later recants and says that he did not really mean it, what would the average parent think of such a parent described? Remember God has left His creation with a moral conscience—not totally reprobate in all one's knowledge of Him or His holy law written (imprinted) upon their hearts. (Romans 1:19-20; 2:12-15)

God not only loves the Believer specifically, individually, and intimately, God also loves all the created world of humanity so much that He would take their punishment. There is no conflict in the omniscient-omnipotent God with such love. There is, however, a conflict with the Calvinists' definitions and explanations. The Biblicist sees no inconsistencies or errors with God loving the world at large and His believers.

The Conflict with God's Sovereignty

When one brings up the conflict with God's sovereignty, really strikes at the core of the Calvinist system. No one can ever make God less sovereign. He does as He pleases. He works His will regardless of Man's will. He reigns supreme above all His creation.

Those are facts as the Scriptures reveal them. Wherein lies the conflict? It is in the understanding or application.

God's sovereignty is not at risk if He allows humanity to have a legitimate will and choice. His sovereignty is not infringed upon if His Spirit draws people to Christ and they resist or reject Him. The Lord's sovereign plan is not upset if all people receive a call to Salvation, but only the willing respond to receiving the predetermined promised security and benefits. The Lord's sovereign grace does not fall if the children of the redeemed do not get saved, nor is it a breach of any promise.

Furthermore, God's sovereignty does not capitulate if He does not regenerate people to advance to new life so someday they choose a new life. Nor can it be said the Lord's sovereign purposes and plans are destroyed if the Calvinist's views on decrees, election, predestination, foreknowledge, depravity, the scope of the atonement, or the promise of the saint's preserving, works-keeping salvation are not quite accurate.

The Biblicist balances all of those ideas in the sovereign omniscience of God. They have no problem with God's grace and the human responsibility of free choice. The Biblicist balances those mutual truths with a God Whom "all things are possible" or Who is able to "work all things together."

The Conflict of Practical Application

The Arminian witnesses the Gospel because his salvation may be at risk. That is pragmatism! The Biblicist witnesses because of the Judgment Seat of Christ and the love of God constrains him. The Calvinist witnesses to perhaps find the Elect who are going to get saved no matter what. They also witness out of some sense of obedience. That is somewhat a measure of contorted altruism. Nevertheless, Christ is preached.

The practicality of the necessity of witnessing or motivation is greatly diminished for the Calvinist. Serving or worshipping becomes introspective fellowshipping awaiting the fellow potential elect. It is no surprise that with the "New Calvinist" the contemplative movement, or emergent church, or house church movement, or seeker centers are very popular today. There is more of an emphasis on "me" as they seek Him. Who needs personal or Ecclesiastical separation?

Another reality is the lack of revival. That subject has always been to the Calvinist either schizophrenic, ignored, or a mystery. In other words, the Calvinist who evangelizes heartily and rejoices over a sinner's conversion does so living a contradiction or paradox. His heart has a passion for the lost sinners and his actions follow through; but their Theology screams "Well, I simply uncovered another Elect who would have been saved anyway."

That is why rationalism, sophistry, or circular reasoning is rampant. It is also why Pentecostalism was an outgrowth of dead orthodoxy in the later 19th century revivals. Those dying conservative mainline churches also gave rise to the Charismatic movement in the 1950's and 1970's. Those people, and likely preachers need to breathe life, fresh air, and fresh souls into their congregation. Today among the Millennials, theological antagonists of the Past have begun to fuse thought among some in the New Calvinist movement, especially with

Charismatics, worldly culture, New Evangelicals or even Roman Catholics.

Consider some of the following thoughts by the Calvinist Jeremy Walker, who noted some dangerous trends he has observed in what is called "New Calvinism":

> So with regards to worship, if we accept that we are always worshipping God and all of culture is up for grabs, there is no needed distinction between the sacred and the profane. That also bleeds over into evangelism because the issue becomes a matter of finding that which attracts people, whatever seems to work.

> It is also worth noting that this appetite for cultural and often academic engagement (which often becomes a desire or need for acceptance with if not quite applause for the world) (may be eroding other doctrinal distinctives of historic Reformed Christianity.). (Walker, 72)

> The third caution or concern is that many within new Calvinism manifest a troubling approach to holiness. There are two elements here. The first is what I consider to be incipient antinomianism. Antinomianism in this context refers, in essence, to those who do not believe in the abiding validity of the moral law for those who are in Christ Jesus. I call it incipient because it is there in seed form even if it is not yet fully broken out in doctrine or in

> practice. As so often, the fourth commandment—the matter of the new covenant Sabbath, the Lord's day—is usually the first point of contact. Many of the leading lights in the new Calvinist movement would formally embrace or at least align themselves toward what is sometimes called New Covenant Theology. (Walker, 74-75)

I personally believe (at best) this tendency is due to a false or heretical view of Grace. Walker further expressed his concerns over the lack of holiness in the movement:

> A false dichotomy is being established between faith and duty or effort and I think that some of this goes back to Piper's idea that we glorify God by enjoying him forever, that God is most glorified in me when I am most satisfied in him. (Please note that John Piper speaks very definitely of the need to pursue and attain genuine holiness as a part of our being saved, although he seems to resist any language of duty or gratitude in or response to grace.) Indeed, I have begun to see it argued that it is not possible that God should be glorified unless I am being immediately satisfied that if I am not being satisfied, then God cannot be glorified. The focus has ended up on self-satisfaction rather than God-glorification. (Ibid., 77-78)

Walker further makes note concerning the tendency of New Calvinism toward Ecumenicism. That reality, however, began in the 1970's, where New Evangelicals joined New Charismatics from old-line denominations.

> **Ecumenism**-A fourth caution or concern is a potentially dangerous ecumenism. There is a pursuit of unity that may end up being at the expense of truth. Remember that this is an eclectic movement, a spectrum not a monolith. There are men all along the spectrum who do not see eye to eye on certain things. (Walker, 83)

Perhaps one of the greatest theological compromises and confusions among New Calvinists is in the area of Spiritual Gifts. Walker stated the following in reference to the topic:

> **Spiritual Gifts** - Furthermore, there is for many new Calvinists a genuine tension with regard to spiritual gifts. This has been identified even within the movement itself as a potential faultline, a point of division which could cause significant dissension. I think the men who have recognized that tension are right, but the present response is often to keep papering over the cracks even while some are driving in the wedges. (Walker, 92)

> John Piper has asserted via Twitter that "God humbles Charismatics by making their children Calvinists, and Calvinists by making their children speak in tongues." Ahem! This is pertinent especially in the

> UK, and perhaps in other places. As previously mentioned, the new Calvinist spectrum in the US is a broad one. In other places, it can appear narrower. In the UK, expressions of new Calvinism are often Charismatic or at least thoroughly ambivalent with regard to the matter of gifts... (Walker, 95)

Calvinism always arises as a response to theological heresies or empty and shallow evangelism. It also responds to pseudo revivals or Neo Antinomianism Christian behavior. That was often the old Calvinist role in the proverbial swinging pendulum. That is no longer the case with Millennials and New Calvinists. This is exactly the position that the 1970's neo-Evangelical movement wound up. The people of that era began to depart or dismiss any forms of Orthodox Theology in its pursuit of pragmatic evangelism. One certainty remains evident: either notion signals the death of true biblical evangelism, revivals, and sanctification! **That result can never be acceptable to the Biblicist!**

Chapter 10: The Sum of the Whole Matter

In this final summary, one needs to find a balanced approach. All would agree that sin has left humanity physically, mentally, and spiritually deficient. Left to one's self, a person is unable to please or obey God. That deficiency referred to as depravity is categorically different than Satan's deficiency or depravity. With mankind, there is the potential capability to make a viable choice of will—the God Who Biblically offers a real offer to mankind of Salvation.

> *2 Peter 3:9   The Lord is not slack concerning his promise, as some men count slackness; but is longsuffering to us-ward, **not willing that any should perish, but that all should come to repentance**.*

For the Calvinists, that offer will only truly be heard or presented to the Preselected and Predestined. That presentation then occurs when the Lord co-ops their will or regenerates it to choose. That offer may even happen years beforehand. It negates a necessity for a person to choose since they have been regenerated already. This so-called preselection of God does so for His undisclosed pleasure and purpose.

Perhaps most disconcerting is that the non-preselected, in violation of the Old Testament Law and New Testament Grace, will still be responsible for a choice they cannot make. That idea too is a violation of the Law of Equity or Equal Justice. It makes God a respecter of persons. While all this may be steadfastly denied, it remains true.

Leviticus 19:15 Ye shall do no unrighteousness in judgment: thou shalt not respect the person of the poor, nor honour the person of the mighty: but in righteousness shalt thou judge thy neighbour.

Deuteronomy 1:17 Ye shall not respect persons in judgment; but ye shall hear the small as well as the great; ye shall not be afraid of the face of man; for the judgment is God's: and the cause that is too hard for you, bring it unto me, and I will hear it.

Leviticus 19:36 Just balances, just weights, a just ephah, and a just hin, shall ye have: I am the LORD your God, which brought you out of the land of Egypt.

Leviticus 24:20 Breach for breach, eye for eye, tooth for tooth: as he hath caused a blemish in a man, so shall it be done to him again.

Leviticus 24:22 Ye shall have one manner of law, as well for the stranger, as for one of your own country: for I am the LORD your God.

Numbers 15:15-16 One ordinance shall be both for you of the congregation, and also for the stranger that sojourneth with you, an ordinance for ever in your generations: as ye are, so shall the stranger be before the LORD. One law and one manner shall be for you, and for the stranger that sojourneth with you.

Numbers 15:29 Ye shall have one law for him that sinneth through ignorance, both for him that is born among the children of Israel, and for the stranger that sojourneth among them.

Deuteronomy 25:15 But thou shalt have a perfect and just weight, a perfect and just measure shalt thou have: that thy days may be lengthened in the land which the LORD thy God giveth thee.

Acts 10:34 Then Peter opened his mouth, and said, Of a truth I perceive that God is no respecter of persons:

No serious person would ever question God's absolute sovereignty. He does what He will for His own good purposes. His good purposes, however, never negate what he has revealed about His goodness, or love, or grace, and plan.

What is bothersome about the Calvinist's system or philosophy is their tendency to ignore or explain away clear Scriptural statements that contradict them. Equally so is the arrogance of some people in thinking they have the marketplace on God's sovereignty. It could be likened to their own semi-omniscience. Rather than yielding to a God who can make two seemingly opposite truths balance in Him, they limit His choice or ability to their finite understanding.

In point, they have no idea who is elect or saved. Further, those who ascribe to that belief have no idea what is the basis of whom God foreknew, and why or what that really means. They have no idea how, or if it is all a mirage for Man. They have in part, an unbiblical view of predestination, the atonement, depravity, and grace. They will force answers in order to make their Aristotelian system work.

The Biblicist cannot, however. A Biblicist, once comparing all Scriptures about Man, Salvation, the Nature of God and the Godhead must arrive at a declaration. That declaration is: "I cannot know what God *has not* revealed—only what He *has* revealed."

> *Deuteronomy 29:1 These are the words of the covenant, which the LORD commanded Moses to make with the children of Israel in the land of Moab, beside the covenant which he made with them in Horeb.*

If two passages seem to collide, then they are balanced by a merciful, loving God, Who works all things together—not simply for the Believer, but literally all things that were known and knowable. He alone balances the answer to man's corrupt rebellious being, who needs salvation and how all are given a real choice to respond. His love is also upon all the world of man, but inevitably only received by the believer. That is hardly so with people, but with God "all things are possible."

It must also be admitted that the concept of election (choosing) is used foremost as a title for the believer. God's purpose is for salvation and glory.

If election is to salvation for those elected, it also is in contradistinction unto sin and damnation! So one can be elect to salvation *or* sin. In Philosophy, that idea is called a *logical absurdity* or *conflict*. Unfortunately, it is the logical conclusion of such an equation in the Calvinist's philosophical system (no matter how honorable the intent). That conflict also contradicts

Newton's Third Law of Motion with their view of predestination and regeneration. A passive non-action is still an action even if it has negative consequences. One action produces a corresponding opposite reaction. It is also a contradiction to the Second Law of Thermodynamics, in which the changes in the entropy in the universe can never be negative.

So, how should one approach or depart this subject? There is only one way—with grace and love in one's heart and treatment of the brethren. Whether Calvinist, Arminian, or Biblicist, Christians will undoubtedly disagree until all get to Heaven. At risk is the testimony of those who are Christ's in a growing antagonistic world. It is equally important as to *how* a Christian stands when taking their stand.

All three of the aforementioned groups hold to Salvation being by Grace, through faith alone. All three believe that "salvation is of the Lord."

Jonah 2:9 But I will sacrifice unto thee with the voice of thanksgiving; I will pay that that I have vowed. Salvation is of the LORD.

Psalms 3:8 Salvation belongeth unto the LORD: thy blessing is upon thy people. Selah.

Two and a half believe that it is all of God's grace and not of works, or it is all of works.

Romans 11:6 And if by grace, then is it no more of works: otherwise grace is no more grace. But if it be of works, then is it no more grace: otherwise work is no more work.

Even the Arminians basically believe the words of Romans 11:6 except for their position in the *possibility* of a Believer choosing against Christ. That belief contradicts the perseverance or security of the Believer. These Arminians, (like Calvinists), believe they are partners with Christ with a Free Will and Calvinists without one. Either way, both groups must *by works* demonstrate personal holiness or righteousness to prove Salvation. All personal sanctification is dependent on one's will with the Holy Spirit, regardless whether Arminian, Biblicist, or Calvinist. Remember, the Calvinist sees the Holy Spirit not only as the motivation enabler but also the cause and effect of Salvation and or keeping the Elect persevering. Of course, that perspective makes the Holy Spirit co-op human will or cooperative with human will enough to be the first cause. With that idea, the Elect does not truly yield to the Spirit; they merely perform the works of the Spirit.

The Biblicist understands that they always have the responsibility to yield before and after salvation. The onus of responsibility is theirs before and after Salvation.

Romans 6:12-13 Let not sin therefore reign in your mortal body, that ye should obey it in the lusts thereof. Neither yield ye your members as instruments of unrighteousness unto sin: but yield yourselves unto God, as those that are alive from the dead, and your members as instruments of righteousness unto God.

Romans 6:16 Know ye not, that to whom ye yield yourselves servants to obey, his servants ye are to whom ye obey; whether of sin unto death, or of obedience unto righteousness?

Their spiritual condition is always dependent upon a free and true choice. Even in the Old Testament, without the advantage of the indwelling presence of the Holy Spirit in the individual, Joshua challenged the nation and the individual to choose.

> *Joshua 24:15 And if it seem evil unto you to serve the LORD, choose you this day whom ye will serve; whether the gods which your fathers served that were on the other side of the flood, or the gods of the Amorites, in whose land ye dwell: but as for me and my house, we will serve the LORD.*

The new security of salvation is based on the eternal new blood covenant of Jesus and of Grace.

> *Hebrews 10:29 Of how much sorer punishment, suppose ye, shall he be thought worthy, who hath trodden under foot the Son of God, and hath counted the blood of the covenant, wherewith he was sanctified, an unholy thing, and hath done despite unto the Spirit of grace?*

Never is that security of salvation based on the works of righteousness. The importance of understanding that point is emphatic for both the Arminian or the Calvinist.

> *Titus 3:5 Not by works of righteousness which we have done, but according to his mercy he saved us, by the washing of regeneration, and renewing of the Holy Ghost;*

The purpose of understanding these points is so the reader appreciates a deeper security in their salvation, which the consistent Calvinist or Arminian cannot. Those groups can only arrive at a subjective assurance of salvation—and not because the Law is now written "in their hearts" eternally and legally by the New Covenant.

> *Hebrews 10:16 This is the covenant that I will make with them after those days, saith the Lord, I will put my laws into their hearts, and in their minds will I write them;*

I desire that the Biblicist will confidently believe in effectual prayer—that they will not despair that all is fixed, or karma, or theologically random selection, or chance. While no one goes to Hell because they did not pray or witness enough (or at all), individuals do play a role in the unfathomable plan of God. God cares and is responsive to our prayers and our passions for Him and His eternal purposed plan. It does matter!

May the Biblicists be assured that God supremely loves them and is not waiting for them to fail, so He can chasten them or remove their Salvation. His chastening is a reality. It is unique to the individual believer for their maturity. Sometimes it is just a gentle word. No one circumstantially knows the If, When, or Who of God's loving discipline.

> *Hebrews 12:5-11 And ye have forgotten the exhortation which speaketh unto you as unto children, My son, despise not thou the chastening of the Lord, nor faint when thou art rebuked of him: For whom the Lord loveth he chasteneth, and scourgeth every son whom he receiveth. If ye endure chastening, God dealeth with you as with*

sons; for what son is he whom the father chasteneth not? But if ye be without chastisement, whereof all are partakers, then are ye bastards, and not sons. Furthermore we have had fathers of our flesh which corrected us, and we gave them reverence: shall we not much rather be in subjection unto the Father of spirits, and live? For they verily for a few days chastened us after their own pleasure; but he for our profit, that we might be partakers of his holiness. Now no chastening for the present seemeth to be joyous, but grievous: nevertheless afterward it yieldeth the peaceable fruit of righteousness unto them which are exercised thereby.

May the Biblicist also be assured that God truly loves all humanity regardless of whether they accept or reject His grace offer to save. It was demonstrated at Calvary and will be reminded to those rejecters at the Great White Throne Judgment. Our prayers and witnessing do matter and make a difference.

Finally, a person would be wise to remember the admonition of the Psalmist in Psalm 107:8,

Psalms 107:8 Oh that men would praise the LORD for his goodness, and for his wonderful works to the children of men!

Summary

The following summary list of points was discussed in this book. These concluding statements are intended to help the serious reader or thinker. May this inspire the reader to approach the subject of Salvation from a Biblicist viewpoint, uninfluenced by preconceived notions or philosophies.

- God's glory is His primary purpose in His personal revelation.
- Salvation is of the Lord in its origin and purpose in order to bring men back into favor and fellowship with God.
- Salvation is by Grace alone through Christ alone
- Salvation's genuine offer is in some way offered to all humanity and not only a select few. That is also true of the atonement.
- All humanity by God's Holy Spirit's is under Grace's convicting (convincing) influence, and have an opportunity to exercise their will to accept or reject God's grace offer. Man's sin and fallen state are uniquely different from Satan and the fallen angels.
- Predestination is God's guarantee of the full awaited blessings or benefits of grace.
- Election is primarily understood as first, a title for the redeemed; and second, unto a purpose defined by God in Scripture, and perhaps rarely as a method for races, nations, persons.
- Regeneration, as defined or used in Scripture, is the restoring to life that which was dead. It cannot be a process that occurs in the womb or infancy, nor days to years in advance to the so-called Chosen, even if

they do not ever respond to salvation. That is the logical absurdity or heresy of modern Calvinism or New Covenant Calvinism.

- Regeneration must occur either immediately before salvation's request by a helpless yielded sinner; at the indiscernible moment of, or immediately after. The latter, however, is the least favorable of the three. The viability of the latter is based upon God's "draw nigh" Character or statement.

- Salvation is secured eternally for all those who believe or place their faith in Christ's atonement for Man's sin. It is not a reward for those maintaining faith and proper works. It is not simply a perseverance accomplished by the Holy Spirit in us doing some proper works. It is primarily a legal transaction accomplished at Calvary and legally granted upon one's faith in Christ's atonement. The Holy Spirit is given to the Believer to enable them to become God's work. The Holy Spirit becomes the Believers down payment (earnest) and "seal unto the day of Redemption."

- Foreknowledge is simply what God knows in advance. It is not His active ability to force things to happen, so He knows. It is part of the operation of His omniscience working conjunctively with the whole. Anything more than that redefines scripture by imposing a presumed notion.

- Dispensationalism is a Theological system that looks at Scripture and God's plan as He unfolds His revelation. It is not without problems, but it is the least problematic. Its system does not owe allegiance to denominationalism as does the Reformed, Covenant or Augustinian–Aquinas Catholic systems. It also seeks more than any other to interpret Scripture objectively and inductively, literally and symbolically, yet not allegorically. People who ascribe to that system also understand that the infinite God balances all truth—even when a person cannot comprehend His revelation in their system. The dispensationalist accepts this as fact, and not a contradictory attempt to invent explanations to squeeze into their own notions.

Works Cited

Armitage, Baker D.D., LL.D. *A History of the Baptists: Traced By Their Vital Principles and Practices From the Time of Our Lord and Savior Jesus Christ to the Present (1886).* Vol. I. Watertown, WI: Maranatha Baptist Press, 1976.

Atonement. (n.d.). Retrieved June 16, 2017, from https://www.merriam-webster.com/dictionary/atonement

Augustinus, Aurelius. *The City of God Against the Pagans.* Edited by David Knowles. New York, NY: Penguin Books, 1972.

Calvin, John. *Institutes of the Christian Religion.* Translated by Henry Beveridge. 2nd ed. Grand Rapids, MI: WM. B. Eerdman's Publishing Company, 1997.

Chaffer, Lewis Sperry, D.D. *Grace: The Glorious Theme.* 18th ed. Grand Rapids, MI: Zondervan House, 1975.

Charnock, Stephen. *The Doctrine of Regeneration.* Grand Rapids, MI: Evangelical Pr. Baker Book House, 1980.

Clarke, William Newton. *An Outline of Christian Theology.* New York: Charles Scribner's, 1911.

Christian, John I. *History of the Baptist.* Vol I. Bogard Press, Texarkana, AR, 1922.

Elwell, Walter A. "Entry for 'Redeem, Redemption'" *Evangelical Dictionary of Theology.* 1997.

Grace. (n.d.). Retrieved June 16, 2017, from www.biblestudytools.com/dictionaries/bakers-evangelical-dictionary/

Grudem, Wayne. *Systematic Theology.* Grand Rapids, MI: Zondervan House, 1994.

Hunt, Dave. *What Love Is This: Calvinism's Misrepresentation of God.* Bend, OR: Berean Call, 2013.

Justification. (n.d.). *Collins English Dictionary - Complete & Unabridged 10th Edition.* Retrieved June 16, 2017 from Dictionary.com
http://www.dictionary.com/browse/justification

Justification. (n.d.). Retrieved June 16, 2017, from
https://www.merriam-webster.com/dictionary/justification

Koehler, Edward W. A., Rev. *Summary of Christian Doctrine.* 2nd ed. Oakland, CA: Rev Alfred W. Koehler, 1952.

Meeter, H. Henry. *The Basic Ideas of Calvinism.* 5th ed. Grand Rapids: Baker Book House, 1956.

Morgan, Edward S. *The Puritan Dilemma.* Ed. Oscar Hanlin. Glenview, IL & London, England: Scott Foresman, 1958.

Picirilli, Robert E. *Grace, Faith, Free Will: Contrasting Views of Salvation : Calvinism and Arminianism.* Nashville: Randall House Publications, 2002.

Schaeffer, Francis A. *How Should We Then Live?: The Rise and Decline of Western Thought and Culture.* Old Tappan, NJ: F.H. Revell, 1976.

Schaefer, Glenn E. "Atonement" In *Baker's Evangelical Dictionary of Biblical Theology,* edited by Walter A. Elwell. Grand Rapids: Baker Books, 1996.
http://www.biblestudytools.com/ dictionaries/bakers-evangelical-dictionary/

Schaefer, Glenn E. "Grace" In *Baker's Evangelical Dictionary of Biblical Theology,* ed. Walter A. Elwell. Grand Rapids: Baker Books, 1996.
http://www.biblestudytools.com/dictionaries/bakers-evangelical-dictionary/

Schaefer, Glenn E. "Predestination" In *Baker's Evangelical Dictionary of Biblical Theology*, edited by Walter A. Elwell. Grand Rapids: Baker Books, 1996. http://www.biblestudytools.com/dictionaries/bakers-evangelical-dictionary/

Spurgeon, C.H. "*On Particular Redemption,*" Retrieved June 16, 2017 from http://sounddoctrine.net *Answering John 3:16 by Nick Bibile.*

Strong, Augustus Hopkins, D.D., LL.D. *Systematic Theology.* Philadelphia, PA: The Judson Press, 1958.

Strong's Exhaustive Concordance: King James Version
Bible. 1995. Updated ed. La Habra: Lockman Foundation. Retrieved June 16, 2017 from http://www.biblestudytools.com/concordances/strongs-exhaustive-concordance/

Studebaker, Richard F., Ph. D. *Theological Influences on the Church: The Theology of James Arminius.* Bethel College Inc. of Indiana. September 1996. Retrieved June 1, 2016. https://www.bethelcollege.edu/assets/content/mcarchives/pdfs/v4n2p4-17.pdf. Series: Reflections. v.4, no.2, p.4-17

Walker, Jeremy. *The New Calvinism Considered: A Personal and Pastoral Assessment.* Darlington, England: Evangelical Press, 1982. Thomas Nelson Publication.

"What is regeneration according to the Bible?" (n.d.). Retrieved June 16, 2017, from https://www.gotquestions.org/regeneration-Bible.html

Vance, Laurence M. *The Other Side of Calvinism.* Pensacola, FL: Vance Publ., 2007.

Consulted Works

Bancroft, Emery H. *Christian Theology: Systematic and Biblical.*
Grand Rapids, MI: Zondervan House, 1972.

Barker, Harold. *Secure Forever.* 3rd Printing. Neptune, NJ: Loizeaux
Bro., 1957.

Evans, William. *The Great Doctrines of the Bible.* Chicago: Bible
Institute Colportage Assoc., 1939.

Hodge, Rev. Achibald Alexander, D.D. *Commentary on the
Confessions of Faith.* Philadelphia, PA: Philadelphia
Presbyterian Board of Publication, 1869.

Miley, John Rev. D.D., Edited by George R. Crook D.D. and John F
Hurst D.D. *Systematic Theology, Vol I.* New York, NY:
Eaton and Mains; Cincinnati. Jennings and Graham, 1894.

Miley, John Rev. D.D., Edited by George R. Crook D.D. and John F
Hurst D.D. *Systematic Theology, Vol. II.* New York, NY:
Eaton and Mains; Cincinnati. Jennings and Graham, 1894.

Milton, Anthony, Ed. *The British Delegation and the Synod of Dort
(1618-1619).* Church of England Record Society.Rochester,
NY: Boydell Press, 2005.

Pentecost, J. Dwight. *Things Which Become Sound Doctrine.* Grand
Rapids, MI: Zondervan House, 1965.

Pink, Arthur W. *Eternal Security.* 18th Printing. Grand Rapids, MI:
Guardian Press, 1974.

Pink, Arthur Walkington. *The Doctrines of Election and Justification.*
Grand Rapids: Baker Book House, 1974.

Rice, John R. *Hyper-Calvinism: A False Doctrine.* Murfreesboro,
TN: Sword of the Lord, 1970.

Stratemeier, Klaas Jacob., B.A., B.D., Th.D. *The Calvinistic Doctrine of Predestination*. Dubuque, IA: Dubuque Presbyterian, 1948.

Strombeck, J. F. *Disciplined by Grace: Studies in Christian Conduct*. Moline, IL: Strombeck Agency, 1946.

Strombeck, J. F. *Shall Never Perish*. 9th ed. Moline: Strombeck Foundation, Distributed by Dunham Publisher, Findlay, OH 1964.

Sumner, Robert L. *An Examination of Tulip: The Five Points of Calvinism*. Brownsburg, IN: Biblical Evangelism, 1972.

Vos, Geerhardus, PH.D., D.D, *Biblical Theology*. Grand Rapids, MI: Wm. B. Eerdmans, 1954.

Other Books Available

Dr. Tobin has written several other books & booklets. They can be found on his church website at TomahBaptistChurch.com.

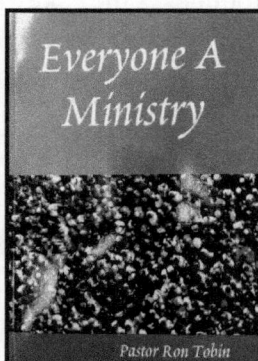

Everyone a Ministry - Dr. Tobin describes how the local church already has all the people and gifts it needs to do the work God has given. Follow the journey and detailed format of a church and their pastor to change their idea of ministry forever. This will be an invaluable resource for any church who wants to see how everyone can become a ministry for Christ in their daily life.

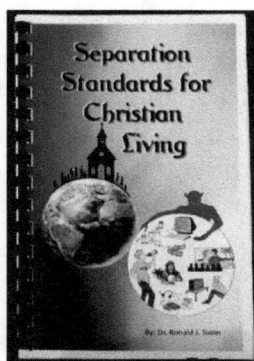

Separation Standards for Christian Living - This book makes an excellent personal or family devotional. It is also greatly used for a large or small group Bible study. Both student or teacher will not be disappointed by the information presented by these, once widely held convictions and standards of Bible believers.

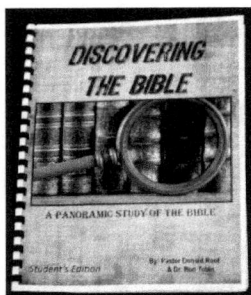

Discovering the Bible (Teacher & Student's Editions) - *Co-Authored with Pastor Don Root,* this 10-lesson study takes a student through the entire Bible with a "fly over the forest" approach rather than an "inspect the bark on the trees" approach. It introduces the key characters, events, and themes of Scripture from a dispensational perspective. The student's edition utilizes fill-in-the-blank, matching, and multiple choice questions to draw the user into an interactive study. Filled with charts, maps, and timelines, the study also weaves in events from secular history to demonstrate that events in Scripture happened in the same world. The Teacher's Edition contains all the correct answers as well as teaching commentary. This makes it an excellent choice for individual discipleship or for the whole church.

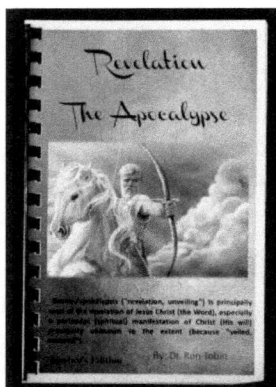

Revelation: The Apocalypse- This series is a wonderful Sunday School or Institute study of the book of Revelation. This has both a separate Teachers and Student edition. The student edition has blanks to fill in that correspond with the answers given in the Teacher's edition. Each page and chapter is filled with amazing color pictures. These pictures can be purchased separately as a PowerPoint Presentation that coordinates with the book chapters.

Principle Lessons for Young Pastors – This is short, but an excellent guide for a new or young pastor, or college student in the early stages of their pastorate. The principles are seldom taught in seminary but confront a pastor early in his ministry. The booklet will make an excellent companion to devotions.

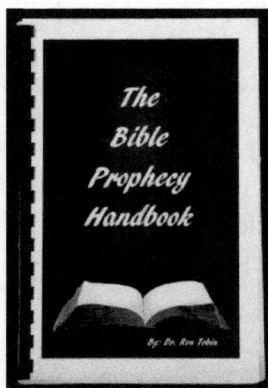

The Bible Prophecy Handbook – This book originated as a Bible Institute course. Later it developed as an adult Bible class and sermon series. The reader will gain invaluable insights into understanding Bible prophecy, past, and future, without wading in too deep of water. It, of course, approaches the subject from a dispensational, pre-Millennial, and pre-Tribulation position.

ABOUT THE AUTHOR

Dr. Tobin has served the Lord for over forty years as a Pastor, as well as an educator in college and high school. His passion is the pastorate where he has been involved in church planting of three works and pastoring existing works. It was as a young elementary student that God began to move in his heart to become a missionary and pastor, even while in a Catholic parochial school.

While under Catholic training (Jesuits, Carmelites, and Augustinians), Dr. Tobin initially began to adopt the Augustinian Theology. However, in the turbulent 1960's he turned briefly in the exact opposite direction rejecting God's rules or religion. Instead, Pastor Tobin turned to Marxism, and through that emptiness, he turned to mysticism.

Gloriously he came to know Jesus Christ in the fall of 1972. Since then, his pursuit has been Christ. It was not difficult to fall back upon Augustinian Theology, now considered Calvinism. After many years of study, however, Dr. Tobin was convinced biblically and practically of the extremes or errors of Calvinism. This is especially true today of the New Covenant (Calvinist) Movement.

Dr. Tobin holds undergraduate degrees in the Bible and several secular studies. He also holds earned MTH and Doctrine of Ministry.

www.ingramcontent.com/pod-product-compliance
Lightning Source LLC
LaVergne TN
LVHW051648080426
835511LV00016B/2554